THE ONE YEAR™

PRAYING THROUGH THE BIBLE FOR YOUR KIDS

Journal

THE ONE YEAR™ PRAYING THROUGH THE BIBLE FOR YOUR KIDS *Journal*

TYNDALE MOMENTUM™

A Tyndale nonfiction imprint

Visit Tyndale online at tyndale.com.

Visit Nancy at nancyguthrie.com.

The One Year Praying through the Bible for Your Kids Journal

Cover design by Libby Dykstra

Interior design by Laura Cruise

For information about special discounts for bulk purchases, please contact Tyndale House Publishers at csresponse@tyndale.com, or call 1-855-277-9400.

ISBN 979-8-4005-1562-0

Printed in India

32 31 30 29 28 27 26
7 6 5 4 3 2 1

HOW TO USE THIS PRAYER JOURNAL

AS A COMPANION TO

THE ONE YEAR PRAYING THROUGH THE BIBLE FOR YOUR KIDS

THERE IS SOMETHING ABOUT PUTTING PEN TO PAPER that helps us turn what we've read in the Bible into meaningful engagement with the God who is speaking to us in Scripture. That's why I've created the prayer journal companion to *The One Year Praying through the Bible for Your Kids* devotional. Each page in this journal begins with a list of that day's Scriptures from the One Year Bible Reading Plan. (You can access that resource using the QR code or URL on page vi.) You'll then find prompts to help you think more deeply about the truths presented in each day's devotional reading, apply their implications more personally, and identify your own desires and needs that should be turned into prayer. Each day you'll be invited to write out prayers specific to your child's situation in light of that day's Bible and devotional reading. And because your life is about more than just you and your child or children, I've included daily space to note other matters for prayer regarding your family, your work, other people, various projects, and the world in which you live.

Similar to the daily readings in the devotional, the prayer prompts in this journal are written with the recognition that some who use it are confident that their child or children have been savingly connected to Christ, while others are hopeful but honestly unsure if this has happened in the lives of one or more of their children. Asking God to save and sanctify us and our children is an appropriate prayer at any point in our lives as salvation has past, present, and future dimensions.

Don't worry if your prayers seem repetitive. Hopefully you'll find fresh language for exploring and expressing your praises, thanksgiving, confession, and requests to God as you go. Even so, the issues at hand or your ongoing needs may remain matters for prayer over time. May this journal help you persevere in prayer over the things that matter most. As you do, I hope you might record how you are seeing the Lord at work in regard to your prayers in the lined pages beginning on page 366 at the back of this journal.

Few of us can keep up with a prayer journal like this without missing some days. When that happens, I encourage you to just pick up where you left off. Praying for our kids is a lifelong endeavor, and we persevere because God has made clear that our prayers matter in the world and in our lives.

I pray this journal will become a treasured depository of your ideas, desires, determinations, and confessions. May it enrich your relationship with God through prayer to him and your relationship with your child or children through praying for them.

Nancy Guthrie

offers.tyndale.com/oy-reading-plan

January 1

GENESIS 1:1–2:25
MATTHEW 1:1–2:12
PSALM 1:1-6
PROVERBS 1:1-6

In the beginning God created the heavens and the earth. The earth was formless and empty, and darkness covered the deep waters. And the Spirit of God was hovering over the surface of the waters. **GENESIS 1:1-2**

Ways I long to see the Creator at work in our home over the coming year:

My prayer for God to fill up our home with his beauty and life:

Other prayer concerns today:

January 2

GENESIS 3:1–4:26
MATTHEW 2:13–3:6
PSALM 2:1-12
PROVERBS 1:7-9

She took some of the fruit and ate it. Then she gave some to her husband, who was with her, and he ate it, too. At that moment their eyes were opened, and they suddenly felt shame at their nakedness. So they sewed fig leaves together to cover themselves. **GENESIS 3:6-7**

My thanksgiving for God's provision of Christ to cover our shame:

My prayer for God to protect my child from rebellion or to bring my child out of rebellion:

Other prayer concerns today:

January 3

GENESIS 5:1–7:24
MATTHEW 3:7–4:11
PSALM 3:1-8
PROVERBS 1:10-19

The LORD observed the extent of human wickedness on the earth, and he saw that everything they thought or imagined was consistently and totally evil. So the LORD was sorry he had ever made them and put them on the earth. It broke his heart. And the LORD said, "I will wipe this human race I have created from the face of the earth. . . ." But Noah found favor with the LORD. **GENESIS 6:5-8**

My gratitude for grace:

My prayer for grace that will change me and my child:

Other prayer concerns today:

GENESIS 8:1–10:32
MATTHEW 4:12-25
PSALM 4:1-8
PROVERBS 1:20-23

January 4

Wisdom shouts in the streets.
She cries out in the public square. . . .
Come and listen to my counsel.
I'll share my heart with you
and make you wise.
PROVERBS 1:20, 23

My desire for wisdom:

My prayer for my child to choose the path that leads to life:

Other prayer concerns today:

January 5

GENESIS 11:1–13:4
MATTHEW 5:1-26
PSALM 5:1-12
PROVERBS 1:24-28

The LORD had said to Abram, "Leave your native country, your relatives, and your father's family, and go to the land that I will show you. I will make you into a great nation. I will bless you and make you famous, and you will be a blessing to others. I will bless those who bless you and curse those who treat you with contempt. All the families on earth will be blessed through you." **GENESIS 12:1-3**

My desires for my child:

My prayer for my child's life to be a work of God's grace:

Other prayer concerns today:

GENESIS 13:5–15:21
MATTHEW 5:27-48
PSALM 6:1-10
PROVERBS 1:29-33

January 6

The LORD took Abram outside and said to him, "Look up into the sky and count the stars if you can. That's how many descendants you will have!" And Abram believed the LORD, and the LORD counted him as righteous because of his faith. **GENESIS 15:5-6**

My gratitude for the righteousness of Christ given as a gift:

My prayer for my child to have saving faith:

Other prayer concerns today:

January 7

GENESIS 16:1–18:15
MATTHEW 6:1-24
PSALM 7:1-17
PROVERBS 2:1-5

Our Father in heaven,
may your name be kept holy.
May your Kingdom come soon.
May your will be done on earth,
as it is in heaven.
Give us today the food we need,
and forgive us our sins,
as we have forgiven those who sin against us.
And don't let us yield to temptation,
but rescue us from the evil one.

MATTHEW 6:9-13

Ways we might nurture more authentic and meaningful family prayer times:

The Lord's Prayer personalized for our family:

Other prayer concerns today:

GENESIS 18:16–19:38
MATTHEW 6:25–7:14
PSALM 8:1-9
PROVERBS 2:6-15

January 8

When Lot still hesitated, the angels seized his hand and the hands of his wife and two daughters and rushed them to safety outside the city, for the LORD was merciful. **GENESIS 19:16**

Ways we may have become desensitized to sin and evil in our home:

My prayer for eyes to see hidden danger and ways we compromise:

Other prayer concerns today:

January 9

GENESIS 20:1–22:24
MATTHEW 7:15-29
PSALM 9:1-12
PROVERBS 2:16-22

The LORD kept his word and did for Sarah exactly what he had promised. She became pregnant, and she gave birth to a son for Abraham in his old age. This happened at just the time God had said it would. **GENESIS 21:1-2**

Things I want to trust God for that seem impossible right now:

My prayer for God to create spiritual life out of spiritual death:

Other prayer concerns today:

January 10

GENESIS 23:1–24:51
MATTHEW 8:1-17
PSALM 9:13-20
PROVERBS 3:1-6

Suddenly, a man with leprosy approached him and knelt before him. "Lord," the man said, "if you are willing, you can heal me and make me clean." Jesus reached out and touched him. "I am willing," he said. "Be healed!" And instantly the leprosy disappeared. **MATTHEW 8:2-3**

Areas in which we need Christ's healing touch:

My prayer for spiritual health and wholeness:

Other prayer concerns today:

January 11

GENESIS 24:52–26:16
MATTHEW 8:18-34
PSALM 10:1-15
PROVERBS 3:7-8

"Look, I'm dying of starvation!" said Esau. "What good is my birthright to me now?" But Jacob said, "First you must swear that your birthright is mine." So Esau swore an oath, thereby selling all his rights as the firstborn to his brother, Jacob. Then Jacob gave Esau some bread and lentil stew. Esau ate the meal, then got up and left. He showed contempt for his rights as the firstborn. **GENESIS 25:32-34**

Ways I might help my child value his or her heavenly inheritance:

My prayer for eyes of faith to see the incredible worth of our eternal inheritance in Christ:

Other prayer concerns today:

January 12

GENESIS 26:17–27:46
MATTHEW 9:1-17
PSALM 10:16-18
PROVERBS 3:9-10

"Is it easier to say 'Your sins are forgiven,' or 'Stand up and walk'? So I will prove to you that the Son of Man has the authority on earth to forgive sins." Then Jesus turned to the paralyzed man and said, "Stand up, pick up your mat, and go home!" And the man jumped up and went home!

MATTHEW 9:5-7

Specific sins I could ask forgiveness for in front of my children to demonstrate that we all need forgiveness:

My prayer of gratitude for God's generous forgiveness:

Other prayer concerns today:

January 13

GENESIS 28:1–29:35
MATTHEW 9:18-38
PSALM 11:1-7
PROVERBS 3:11-12

When he saw the crowds, he had compassion on them because they were confused and helpless, like sheep without a shepherd. He said to his disciples, "The harvest is great, but the workers are few. So pray to the Lord who is in charge of the harvest; ask him to send more workers into his fields." **MATTHEW 9:36-38**

Ways I might encourage compassion in my child for those who are like sheep without a shepherd:

My prayer of surrender of myself and my child to God's purposes:

Other prayer concerns today:

January 14

GENESIS 30:1–31:16
MATTHEW 10:1-23
PSALM 12:1-8
PROVERBS 3:13-15

When Rachel saw that she wasn't having any children for Jacob, she became jealous of her sister. She pleaded with Jacob, "Give me children, or I'll die!" **GENESIS 30:1**

Things I am tempted to think I must have to be happy apart from Christ:

My prayer to surrender having the family I think I must have to be happy:

Other prayer concerns today:

January 15

GENESIS 31:17–32:12
MATTHEW 10:24–11:6
PSALM 13:1-6
PROVERBS 3:16-18

If you love your father or mother more than you love me, you are not worthy of being mine; or if you love your son or daughter more than me, you are not worthy of being mine. If you refuse to take up your cross and follow me, you are not worthy of being mine. If you cling to your life, you will lose it; but if you give up your life for me, you will find it. **MATTHEW 10:37-39**

Ways I might encourage my child to love Jesus supremely:

My prayer that my child would love Jesus more than anyone:

Other prayer concerns today:

January 16

GENESIS 32:13–34:31
MATTHEW 11:7-30
PSALM 14:1-7
PROVERBS 3:19-20

This left Jacob all alone in the camp, and a man came and wrestled with him until the dawn began to break. When the man saw that he would not win the match, he touched Jacob's hip and wrenched it out of its socket. Then the man said, "Let me go, for the dawn is breaking!" But Jacob said, "I will not let you go unless you bless me." **GENESIS 32:24-26**

Struggles my child has faced or might face that could result in greater desire for and dependence on Christ:

My prayer for my child to emerge from life's struggles having been pressed more deeply into Christ:

Other prayer concerns today:

January 17

GENESIS 35:1–36:43
MATTHEW 12:1-21
PSALM 15:1-5
PROVERBS 3:21-26

These are the names of the twelve sons of Jacob: The sons of Leah were Reuben (Jacob's oldest son), Simeon, Levi, Judah, Issachar, and Zebulun. The sons of Rachel were Joseph and Benjamin. The sons of Bilhah, Rachel's servant, were Dan and Naphtali. The sons of Zilpah, Leah's servant, were Gad and Asher. **GENESIS 35:22-26**

Praise to God for welcoming flagrant but forgiven sinners into his family:

My prayer that my child desire to be a part of God's imperfect family:

Other prayer concerns today:

January 18

GENESIS 37:1–38:30
MATTHEW 12:22-45
PSALM 16:1-11
PROVERBS 3:27-32

Jacob loved Joseph more than any of his other children because Joseph had been born to him in his old age. So one day Jacob had a special gift made for Joseph—a beautiful robe. But his brothers hated Joseph because their father loved him more than the rest of them. They couldn't say a kind word to him. **GENESIS 37:3-4**

My tendencies, sins, failures, and blind spots that I'm afraid might adversely impact my child:

My prayer for God to use even my sins and failures to accomplish his good purposes in my child's life:

Other prayer concerns today:

January 19

GENESIS 39:1–41:16
MATTHEW 12:46–13:23
PSALM 17:1-15
PROVERBS 3:33-35

"Come and sleep with me," she demanded. But Joseph refused. "Look," he told her, "my master trusts me with everything in his entire household. No one here has more authority than I do. He has held back nothing from me except you, because you are his wife. How could I do such a wicked thing? It would be a great sin against God." **GENESIS 39:7-9**

Temptations I fear may overtake my child:

My prayer for my child to develop a resolve not to sin when tempted:

Other prayer concerns today:

January 20

GENESIS 41:17–42:17
MATTHEW 13:24-46
PSALM 18:1-15
PROVERBS 4:1-6

The Kingdom of Heaven is like a treasure that a man discovered hidden in a field. In his excitement, he hid it again and sold everything he owned to get enough money to buy the field. Again, the Kingdom of Heaven is like a merchant on the lookout for choice pearls. When he discovered a pearl of great value, he sold everything he owned and bought it! **MATTHEW 13:44-46**

Things my child might need to let go of to have more of Christ:

My prayer to be willing to see my child lose out on worldly things to gain Christ:

Other prayer concerns today:

January 21

GENESIS 42:18–43:34
MATTHEW 13:47–14:12
PSALM 18:16-36
PROVERBS 4:7-10

He reached down from heaven and rescued me;
he drew me out of deep waters.
He rescued me from my powerful enemies,
from those who hated me and were too strong for me.
They attacked me at a moment when I was in distress,
but the LORD supported me.
He led me to a place of safety;
he rescued me because he delights in me.
PSALM 18:16-19

Ways I've experienced God's rescue:

My prayer for my child to experience divine rescue and support in his or her struggles:

Other prayer concerns today:

January 22

GENESIS 44:1–45:28
MATTHEW 14:13-36
PSALM 18:37-50
PROVERBS 4:11-13

I cannot go back to my father without the boy. Our father's life is bound up in the boy's life. If he sees that the boy is not with us, our father will die. We, your servants, will indeed be responsible for sending that grieving, white-haired man to his grave. My lord, I guaranteed to my father that I would take care of the boy. I told him, "If I don't bring him back to you, I will bear the blame forever." So please, my lord, let me stay here as a slave instead of the boy, and let the boy return with his brothers. For how can I return to my father if the boy is not with me? I couldn't bear to see the anguish this would cause my father! **GENESIS 44:30-34**

Ways I pray my child will become more like Christ over his or her lifetime:

My prayer to love my child fiercely without making him or her my life:

Other prayer concerns today:

January 23

GENESIS 46:1–47:31
MATTHEW 15:1-28
PSALM 19:1-14
PROVERBS 4:14-19

You hypocrites! Isaiah was right when he prophesied about you, for he wrote, "These people honor me with their lips, but their hearts are far from me." . . . The words you speak come from the heart—that's what defiles you. For from the heart come evil thoughts, murder, adultery, all sexual immorality, theft, lying, and slander. **MATTHEW 15:7-8, 18-19**

Ways my child might see a disconnect between the faith I talk about and the way I live:

My prayer for my child to develop sincere faith and a soft heart:

Other prayer concerns today:

GENESIS 48:1–49:33
MATTHEW 15:29–16:12
PSALM 20:1-9
PROVERBS 4:20-27

January 24

Guard your heart above all else,
for it determines the course of your life.
Avoid all perverse talk;
stay away from corrupt speech.
Look straight ahead,
and fix your eyes on what lies before you.
Mark out a straight path for your feet;
stay on the safe path.
Don't get sidetracked;
keep your feet from following evil.
PROVERBS 4:23-27

My fears of ways my child might get off track from following Christ:

My prayer for every part of my child's body to be dedicated and disciplined toward pleasing God:

Other prayer concerns today:

January 25

GENESIS 50:1—EXODUS 2:10
MATTHEW 16:13–17:9
PSALM 21:1-13
PROVERBS 5:1-6

Then Jesus said to his disciples, "If any of you wants to be my follower, you must give up your own way, take up your cross, and follow me. If you try to hang on to your life, you will lose it. But if you give up your life for my sake, you will save it. And what do you benefit if you gain the whole world but lose your own soul?" **MATTHEW 16:24-26**

Ways I can help my child see what Christ offers to us in contrast to the way the world takes from us:

My prayer for my child to see the temporal value of worldly things and the eternal value of having Christ:

Other prayer concerns today:

January 26

EXODUS 2:11–3:22
MATTHEW 17:10-27
PSALM 22:1-18
PROVERBS 5:7-14

The LORD told him, "I have certainly seen the oppression of my people in Egypt. I have heard their cries of distress because of their harsh slave drivers. Yes, I am aware of their suffering. So I have come down to rescue them from the power of the Egyptians and lead them out of Egypt into their own fertile and spacious land. . . . When you have brought the people out of Egypt, you will worship God at this very mountain." **EXODUS 3:7-8, 12**

Ways I'm sometimes afraid our family and family members can never change:

My prayer for divine rescue and redemption in our family:

Other prayer concerns today:

January 27

EXODUS 4:1–5:21
MATTHEW 18:1-20
PSALM 22:19-31
PROVERBS 5:15-21

About that time the disciples came to Jesus and asked, "Who is greatest in the Kingdom of Heaven?" Jesus called a little child to him and put the child among them. Then he said, "I tell you the truth, unless you turn from your sins and become like little children, you will never get into the Kingdom of Heaven. So anyone who becomes as humble as this little child is the greatest in the Kingdom of Heaven." **MATTHEW 18:1-4**

Ways I sense my own neediness in parenting:

My prayer for the humility to live before my child with childlike trust in God:

Other prayer concerns today:

EXODUS 5:22–7:25
MATTHEW 18:21–19:12
PSALM 23:1-6
PROVERBS 5:22-23

January 28

The LORD *is my shepherd;*
I have all that I need.
PSALM 23:1

Ways I'm grateful to know that Jesus is shepherding our family:

My prayer for my child to welcome the protection and provision of the Good Shepherd:

Other prayer concerns today:

January 29

EXODUS 8:1–9:35
MATTHEW 19:13-30
PSALM 24:1-10
PROVERBS 6:1-5

Someone came to Jesus with this question: "Teacher, what good deed must I do to have eternal life?" . . . Jesus told him, "If you want to be perfect, go and sell all your possessions and give the money to the poor, and you will have treasure in heaven. Then come, follow me." But when the young man heard this, he went away sad, for he had many possessions. **MATTHEW 19:16, 21-22**

My dreams for my child's life:

My prayer for my child to be spiritually rich, genuinely spiritual, and a humble servant:

Other prayer concerns today:

January 30

EXODUS 10:1–12:13
MATTHEW 20:1-28
PSALM 25:1-15
PROVERBS 6:6-11

The mother of James and John, the sons of Zebedee, came to Jesus with her sons. She knelt respectfully to ask a favor. "What is your request?" he asked. She replied, "In your Kingdom, please let my two sons sit in places of honor next to you, one on your right and the other on your left." **MATTHEW 20:20-21**

Ways I want my ambitions for my child to be shaped by the Kingdom of God:

My prayer for my ambitions for myself and my child to be purified by the Spirit of Christ:

Other prayer concerns today:

January 31

EXODUS 12:14–13:16
MATTHEW 20:29–21:22
PSALM 25:16-22
PROVERBS 6:12-15

Moses called all the elders of Israel together and said to them, "Go, pick out a lamb or young goat for each of your families, and slaughter the Passover animal. Drain the blood into a basin. Then take a bundle of hyssop branches and dip it into the blood. Brush the hyssop across the top and sides of the doorframes of your houses. And no one may go out through the door until morning. For the LORD *will pass through the land to strike down the Egyptians. But when he sees the blood on the top and sides of the doorframe, the* LORD *will pass over your home. He will not permit his death angel to enter your house and strike you down."* **EXODUS 12:21-23**

My prayer of petition for my child to take refuge in the blood of the Lamb of God, Jesus Christ:

My prayer of gratitude for the blood of Christ that covers every sin:

Other prayer concerns today:

EXODUS 13:17–15:18
MATTHEW 21:23-46
PSALM 26:1-12
PROVERBS 6:16-19

February 1

There are six things the LORD hates—
no, seven things he detests:
haughty eyes,
a lying tongue,
hands that kill the innocent,
a heart that plots evil,
feet that race to do wrong,
a false witness who pours out lies,
a person who sows discord in a family.
PROVERBS 6:16-19

Ways I long for the grace of God to change me and my children:

My prayer for me and my children to hate what God hates and love what he loves:

Other prayer concerns today:

February 2

EXODUS 15:19–17:7
MATTHEW 22:1-33
PSALM 27:1-6
PROVERBS 6:20-26

The LORD said to Moses, "I have heard the Israelites' complaints. Now tell them, 'In the evening you will have meat to eat, and in the morning you will have all the bread you want. Then you will know that I am the LORD your God.'" **EXODUS 16:11-12**

What my child might have heard me complain or grumble about lately:

My prayer for our family to be marked by gratitude instead of grumbling:

Other prayer concerns today:

EXODUS 17:8–19:15
MATTHEW 22:34–23:12
PSALM 27:7-14
PROVERBS 6:27-35

February 3

One of them, an expert in religious law, tried to trap him with this question: "Teacher, which is the most important commandment in the law of Moses?" Jesus replied, "'You must love the LORD your God with all your heart, all your soul, and all your mind.' This is the first and greatest commandment. A second is equally important: 'Love your neighbor as yourself.'" **MATTHEW 22:35-39**

Things I need to talk about less and things I need to talk about more:

My prayer to love the Lord with all of my heart, soul, and mind:

Other prayer concerns today:

February 4

EXODUS 19:16–21:21
MATTHEW 23:13-39
PSALM 28:1-9
PROVERBS 7:1-5

When the people heard the thunder and the loud blast of the ram's horn, and when they saw the flashes of lightning and the smoke billowing from the mountain, they stood at a distance, trembling with fear. . . . "Don't be afraid," Moses answered them, "for God has come in this way to test you, and so that your fear of him will keep you from sinning!" **EXODUS 20:18, 20**

Commandments I have broken that deserve God's fiery judgment:

My prayer of thanksgiving for the active obedience of Christ that will enable me to stand before a holy God:

Other prayer concerns:

February 5

EXODUS 21:22–23:13
MATTHEW 24:1-28
PSALM 29:1-11
PROVERBS 7:6-23

So she seduced him with her pretty speech
and enticed him with her flattery.
He followed her at once,
like an ox going to the slaughter.
He was like a stag caught in a trap,
awaiting the arrow that would pierce its heart.
He was like a bird flying into a snare,
little knowing it would cost him his life.
PROVERBS 7:21-23

My fears about the sexual temptations my child faces:

My prayer for wisdom to know how to guide my child toward sexual purity and seek forgiveness for any sexual failure:

Other prayer concerns today:

February 6

EXODUS 23:14–25:40
MATTHEW 24:29-51
PSALM 30:1-12
PROVERBS 7:24-27

Moses went down to the people and repeated all the instructions and regulations the LORD had given him. All the people answered with one voice, "We will do everything the LORD has commanded." **EXODUS 24:3**

Good intentions I've had but failed to follow through on:

My prayer for the Spirit to give me the desire and the power to live in the way I know pleases the Lord:

Other prayer concerns today:

February 7

EXODUS 26:1–27:21
MATTHEW 25:1-30
PSALM 31:1-8
PROVERBS 8:1-11

The Kingdom of Heaven can be illustrated by the story of a man going on a long trip. He called together his servants and entrusted his money to them while he was gone. He gave five bags of silver to one, two bags of silver to another, and one bag of silver to the last—dividing it in proportion to their abilities. He then left on his trip. **MATTHEW 25:14-15**

Abilities, opportunities, experiences, and advantages I've been given that I can leverage for the Kingdom of God:

My prayer for me and my child to invest what we've been entrusted with to build Christ's Kingdom, not our own:

Other prayer concerns today:

February 8

EXODUS 28:1-43
MATTHEW 25:31–26:13
PSALM 31:9-18
PROVERBS 8:12-13

I am trusting you, O LORD,
saying, "You are my God!"
My future is in your hands.
PSALM 31:14-15

Aspects of my child's life and future I want to trust God with:

My prayer casting all my anxieties about my child's life on the God who holds the future:

Other prayer concerns today:

EXODUS 29:1–30:10
MATTHEW 26:14-46
PSALM 31:19-24
PROVERBS 8:14-26

February 9

He went on a little farther and bowed with his face to the ground, praying, "My Father! If it is possible, let this cup of suffering be taken away from me. Yet I want your will to be done, not mine." **MATTHEW 26:39**

Aspects of God's plan for my family's life I have struggled to submit to:

My prayer to welcome God's will to be done in our family:

Other prayer concerns today:

February 10

EXODUS 30:11–31:18
MATTHEW 26:47-68
PSALM 32:1-11
PROVERBS 8:27-32

Oh, what joy for those
whose disobedience is forgiven,
whose sin is put out of sight! . . .
When I refused to confess my sin,
my body wasted away,
and I groaned all day long.
Day and night your hand of discipline was heavy on me.
My strength evaporated like water in the summer heat.
PSALM 32:1, 3-4

Sins I've been convicted of and found joy in being forgiven for:

My prayer for me and my child to welcome rather than ignore conviction of sin so that we can confess and be forgiven:

Other prayer concerns today:

February 11

EXODUS 32:1–33:23
MATTHEW 26:69–27:14
PSALM 33:1-11
PROVERBS 8:33-36

The LORD said to Moses, ". . . Go up to this land that flows with milk and honey. But I will not travel among you, for you are a stubborn and rebellious people. If I did, I would surely destroy you along the way." **EXODUS 33:1, 3**

Ways our family can demonstrate that we want the presence of God as much as we want the blessings of God:

My prayer that our family's desire for and awareness of God's presence in our home would increase:

Other prayer concerns today:

February 12

EXODUS 34:1–35:9
MATTHEW 27:15-31
PSALM 33:12-22
PROVERBS 9:1-6

Yahweh! The LORD!
The God of compassion and mercy!
I am slow to anger
and filled with unfailing love and faithfulness.
I lavish unfailing love to a thousand generations.
I forgive iniquity, rebellion, and sin.
But I do not excuse the guilty.
I lay the sins of the parents upon their children and grandchildren;
the entire family is affected—
even children in the third and fourth generations.
EXODUS 34:6-7

Patterns or tendencies I don't want to pass along to my children:

My prayer for the compassion and mercy of God to loom larger in the lives of my children than any consequences of my own sin:

Other prayer concerns today:

EXODUS 35:10–36:38
MATTHEW 27:32-66
PSALM 34:1-10
PROVERBS 9:7-8

February 13

I prayed to the LORD, and he answered me.
He freed me from all my fears.
Those who look to him for help will be radiant with joy;
no shadow of shame will darken their faces.

PSALM 34:4-5

Fears about my family and my child I need to be freed from:

My prayer for grace to look to the Lord for help rather than focus on my fears:

Other prayer concerns today:

February 14

EXODUS 37:1–38:31
MATTHEW 28:1-20
PSALM 34:11-22
PROVERBS 9:9-10

Jesus came and told his disciples, "I have been given all authority in heaven and on earth. Therefore, go and make disciples of all the nations, baptizing them in the name of the Father and the Son and the Holy Spirit. Teach these new disciples to obey all the commands I have given you. And be sure of this: I am with you always, even to the end of the age." **MATTHEW 28:18-20**

Ways we are or could follow the command of Jesus to make disciples:

My prayer for our family to grow in our passion for being a part of this mission of God:

Other prayer concerns today:

February 15

EXODUS 39:1–40:38
MARK 1:1-28
PSALM 35:1-16
PROVERBS 9:11-12

The craftsmen made beautiful sacred garments of blue, purple, and scarlet cloth—clothing for Aaron to wear while ministering in the Holy Place, just as the LORD had commanded Moses. . . . The ephod consisted of two pieces, front and back, joined at the shoulders with two shoulder-pieces. . . . They mounted the two onyx stones in settings of gold filigree. The stones were engraved with the names of the tribes of Israel, just as a seal is engraved. He fastened these stones on the shoulder-pieces of the ephod as a reminder that the priest represents the people of Israel. **EXODUS 39:1, 4, 6-7**

Burdens I can be sure my Great High Priest is carrying even now into the presence of God:

My prayer of gratitude that I don't bear the full load of the needs of my children:

Other prayer concerns today:

February 16

LEVITICUS 1:1–3:17
MARK 1:29–2:12
PSALM 35:17-28
PROVERBS 9:13-18

The woman named Folly is brash.
She is ignorant and doesn't know it.
She sits in her doorway
on the heights overlooking the city.
She calls out to men going by
who are minding their own business.
"Come in with me," she urges the simple.
To those who lack good judgment, she says,
"Stolen water is refreshing;
food eaten in secret tastes the best!"
But little do they know that the dead are there.
Her guests are in the depths of the grave.
PROVERBS 9:13-18

Folly or foolishness I pray my child will avoid:

My prayer for my child to keep choosing the path that leads to life and joy in Christ:

Other prayer concerns today:

February 17

LEVITICUS 4:1–5:19
MARK 2:13–3:6
PSALM 36:1-12
PROVERBS 10:1-2

When you become aware of your guilt in any of these ways, you must confess your sin. Then you must bring to the L*ORD as the penalty for your sin a female from the flock, either a sheep or a goat. This is a sin offering with which the priest will purify you from your sin, making you right with the* L*ORD.* **LEVITICUS 5:5-6**

Ways we might emphasize the gravity of sin in our family while also relishing forgiveness through Christ:

My prayer of gratitude for the once-for-all sacrifice of Jesus that makes forgiveness available to our family:

Other prayer concerns today:

February 18

LEVITICUS 6:1–7:27
MARK 3:7-30
PSALM 37:1-11
PROVERBS 10:3-4

Trust in the LORD and do good.
Then you will live safely in the land and prosper.
Take delight in the LORD,
and he will give you your heart's desires.
PSALM 37:3-4

Ways I could nurture my own delight in the Lord:

My prayer for the Spirit to sanctify and shape my desires for my child:

Other prayer concerns today:

February 19

LEVITICUS 7:28–9:6
MARK 3:31–4:25
PSALM 37:12-29
PROVERBS 10:5

Jesus' mother and brothers came to see him. They stood outside and sent word for him to come out and talk with them. There was a crowd sitting around Jesus, and someone said, "Your mother and your brothers are outside asking for you." Jesus replied, "Who is my mother? Who are my brothers?" Then he looked at those around him and said, "Look, these are my mother and brothers. Anyone who does God's will is my brother and sister and mother." **MARK 3:31-35**

Outsiders I pray will become insiders to the grace of Jesus:

My prayer for those who have not yet believed to come to genuine faith:

Other prayer concerns today:

February 20

LEVITICUS 9:7–10:20
MARK 4:26–5:20
PSALM 37:30-40
PROVERBS 10:6-7

Aaron's sons Nadab and Abihu put coals of fire in their incense burners and sprinkled incense over them. In this way, they disobeyed the LORD by burning before him the wrong kind of fire, different than he had commanded. **LEVITICUS 10:1**

Spiritual fruit in my child's life I'm tempted to take credit for and sin I'm tempted to blame myself for:

My prayer for God to save me from thinking my child's spiritual condition is up to me:

Other prayer concerns today:

LEVITICUS 11:1–12:8
MARK 5:21-43
PSALM 38:1-22
PROVERBS 10:8-9

February 21

By these instructions you will know what is unclean and clean, and which animals may be eaten and which may not be eaten. **LEVITICUS 11:47**

Aspects of my life I long to be made perfectly clean:

My prayer for God to make me clean in these areas:

Other prayer concerns today:

February 22

LEVITICUS 13:1-29
MARK 6:1-29
PSALM 39:1-13
PROVERBS 10:10

People who wink at wrong cause trouble,
but a bold reproof promotes peace.
PROVERBS 10:10

Situations in which my child may need bold reproof:

My prayer for the will and courage to lovingly reprove my child when needed:

Other prayer concerns today:

February 23

LEVITICUS 14:1-57
MARK 6:30-56
PSALM 40:1-10
PROVERBS 10:11-12

Late that night, the disciples were in their boat in the middle of the lake, and Jesus was alone on land. He saw that they were in serious trouble, rowing hard and struggling against the wind and waves. About three o'clock in the morning Jesus came toward them, walking on the water. He intended to go past them, but when they saw him walking on the water, they cried out in terror, thinking he was a ghost. They were all terrified when they saw him. But Jesus spoke to them at once. "Don't be afraid," he said. "Take courage! I am here!" Then he climbed into the boat, and the wind stopped. **MARK 6:47-51**

Problems I want to invite Jesus into rather than try to fix on my own:

My prayer inviting Jesus into the challenges facing our family:

Other prayer concerns today:

February 24

LEVITICUS 15:1–16:28
MARK 7:1-23
PSALM 40:11-17
PROVERBS 10:13-14

It's not what goes into your body that defiles you; you are defiled by what comes from your heart. **MARK 7:15**

Matters of the heart I'm concerned about:

My prayer for myself and my child to be cleansed of the sins that Jesus said defile a person:

Other prayer concerns today:

February 25

LEVITICUS 16:29–18:30
MARK 7:24–8:10
PSALM 41:1-13
PROVERBS 10:15-16

A woman who had heard about him came and fell at his feet. Her little girl was possessed by an evil spirit, and she begged him to cast out the demon from her daughter. **MARK 7:25-26**

Needs I'm desperate for God to meet, knowing he is the only one who can:

My prayer of desperation for God to protect our family from evil:

Other prayer concerns today:

February 26

LEVITICUS 19:1–20:21
MARK 8:11-38
PSALM 42:1-11
PROVERBS 10:17

Calling the crowd to join his disciples, he said, "If any of you wants to be my follower, you must give up your own way, take up your cross, and follow me. If you try to hang on to your life, you will lose it. But if you give up your life for my sake and for the sake of the Good News, you will save it." **MARK 8:34-35**

Ambitions I have for my child that need to be submitted to the call of Christ:

My prayer for my child to take up a cross and follow Jesus:

Other prayer concerns today:

February 27

LEVITICUS 20:22–22:16
MARK 9:1-29
PSALM 43:1-5
PROVERBS 10:18

"How long has this been happening?" Jesus asked the boy's father. He replied, "Since he was a little boy. The spirit often throws him into the fire or into water, trying to kill him. Have mercy on us and help us, if you can." **MARK 9:21-22**

Things I want to trust God with in a deeper way:

My prayer for intervention and the faith to trust God for it:

Other prayer concerns today:

February 28

LEVITICUS 22:17–23:44
MARK 9:30–10:12
PSALM 44:1-8
PROVERBS 10:19

You have six days each week for your ordinary work, but the seventh day is a Sabbath day of complete rest, an official day for holy assembly. It is the L*ORD's Sabbath day, and it must be observed wherever you live.* **LEVITICUS 23:3**

Adjustments we could make to honor God more fully on his day:

My prayer for our family to grow in our delight of the Sabbath:

Other prayer concerns today:

March 1

LEVITICUS 24:1–25:46
MARK 10:13-31
PSALM 44:9-26
PROVERBS 10:20-21

"Teacher," the man replied, "I've obeyed all these commandments since I was young." Looking at the man, Jesus felt genuine love for him. "There is still one thing you haven't done," he told him. "Go and sell all your possessions and give the money to the poor, and you will have treasure in heaven. Then come, follow me." **MARK 10:20-21**

Passions that drive my behaviors and my child's behaviors:

My prayer for idols in our lives to be exposed and eradicated:

Other prayer concerns today:

March 2

LEVITICUS 25:47–27:13
MARK 10:32-52
PSALM 45:1-17
PROVERBS 10:22

Bartimaeus threw aside his coat, jumped up, and came to Jesus. "What do you want me to do for you?" Jesus asked. "My Rabbi," the blind man said, "I want to see!" **MARK 10:50-51**

Aspects of who Jesus is, what he provides, and what he has done that I want my child to recognize:

My prayer for Jesus to open my child's eyes to see:

Other prayer concerns today:

March 3

LEVITICUS 27:14–NUMBERS 1:54
MARK 11:1-26
PSALM 46:1-11
PROVERBS 10:23

One-tenth of the produce of the land, whether grain from the fields or fruit from the trees, belongs to the L*ORD and must be set apart to him as holy.* **LEVITICUS 27:30**

Ways I can encourage my child to be a cheerful giver:

My prayer for my child to have joy in giving to God and others:

Other prayer concerns today:

March 4

NUMBERS 2:1–3:51
MARK 11:27–12:17
PSALM 47:1-9
PROVERBS 10:24-25

When the storms of life come, the wicked are whirled away,
but the godly have a lasting foundation.
PROVERBS 10:25

Ways our family can build a strong foundation that can withstand the storms of life:

My prayer for my child's life to be built on a strong foundation:

Other prayer concerns today:

March 5

NUMBERS 4:1–5:31
MARK 12:18-37
PSALM 48:1-14
PROVERBS 10:26

One of the teachers of religious law was standing there listening to the debate. He realized that Jesus had answered well, so he asked, "Of all the commandments, which is the most important?" Jesus replied, "The most important commandment is this: 'Listen, O Israel! The LORD our God is the one and only LORD. And you must love the LORD your God with all your heart, all your soul, all your mind, and all your strength.' The second is equally important: 'Love your neighbor as yourself.' No other commandment is greater than these." **MARK 12:28-31**

Ways we can set an example before our children in loving the Lord and loving our neighbors:

My prayer for my child to love the Lord and our neighbors:

Other prayer concerns today:

March 6

NUMBERS 6:1–7:89
MARK 12:38–13:13
PSALM 49:1-20
PROVERBS 10:27-28

Then the LORD said to Moses, "Tell Aaron and his sons to bless the people of Israel with this special blessing: 'May the LORD bless you and protect you. May the LORD smile on you and be gracious to you. May the LORD show you his favor and give you his peace.'" **NUMBERS 6:22-26**

Ways these verses express what it means to be blessed:

My prayer for the Lord to bless our family in these ways:

Other prayer concerns today:

March 7

NUMBERS 8:1–9:23
MARK 13:14-37
PSALM 50:1-23
PROVERBS 10:29-30

On the day the Tabernacle was set up, the cloud covered it. But from evening until morning the cloud over the Tabernacle looked like a pillar of fire. This was the regular pattern—at night the cloud that covered the Tabernacle had the appearance of fire. Whenever the cloud lifted from over the sacred tent, the people of Israel would break camp and follow it. And wherever the cloud settled, the people of Israel would set up camp. **NUMBERS 9:15-17**

Unknowns that I can trust God to guide me through:

My prayer for the Spirit's guidance:

Other prayer concerns today:

March 8

NUMBERS 10:1–11:23
MARK 14:1-21
PSALM 51:1-19
PROVERBS 10:31-32

Then the foreign rabble who were traveling with the Israelites began to crave the good things of Egypt. And the people of Israel also began to complain. "Oh, for some meat!" they exclaimed. "We remember the fish we used to eat for free in Egypt. And we had all the cucumbers, melons, leeks, onions, and garlic we wanted. But now our appetites are gone. All we ever see is this manna!" **NUMBERS 11:4-6**

Cravings that might be causing me to lose sight of God's goodness:

My prayer for contentment with what God graciously provides:

Other prayer concerns today:

March 9

NUMBERS 11:24–13:33
MARK 14:22-52
PSALM 52:1-9
PROVERBS 11:1-3

Peter said to him, "Even if everyone else deserts you, I never will." Jesus replied, "I tell you the truth, Peter—this very night, before the rooster crows twice, you will deny three times that you even know me." "No!" Peter declared emphatically. "Even if I have to die with you, I will never deny you!" And all the others vowed the same. **MARK 14:29-31**

Temptations we need the Lord's strength to keep from falling into:

My prayer for grace and strength to stay alert and be on guard against temptation:

Other prayer concerns today:

March 10

NUMBERS 14:1–15:16
MARK 14:53-72
PSALM 53:1-6
PROVERBS 11:4

God looks down from heaven
on the entire human race;
he looks to see if anyone is truly wise,
if anyone seeks God.
But no, all have turned away;
all have become corrupt.
No one does good,
not a single one!
PSALM 53:2-3

Evidence I long to see in my child's life that he or she is seeking after God:

My prayer of praise that the Savior seeks those who are not seeking him:

Other prayer concerns today:

March 11

NUMBERS 15:17–16:40
MARK 15:1-47
PSALM 54:1-7
PROVERBS 11:5-6

At noon, darkness fell across the whole land until three o'clock. Then at three o'clock Jesus called out with a loud voice, "Eloi, Eloi, lema sabachthani?" *which means "My God, my God, why have you abandoned me?"* **MARK 15:33-34**

Situations in which I can be confident that God has not abandoned me:

My prayer of thanksgiving for the constant gracious presence of God in our lives:

Other prayer concerns today:

March 12

NUMBERS 16:41–18:32
MARK 16:1-20
PSALM 55:1-23
PROVERBS 11:7

The Lord said to Moses: "Place Aaron's staff permanently before the Ark of the Covenant to serve as a warning to rebels. This should put an end to their complaints against me and prevent any further deaths." So Moses did as the Lord commanded him. Then the people of Israel said to Moses, "Look, we are doomed! We are dead! We are ruined! Everyone who even comes close to the Tabernacle of the Lord dies. Are we all doomed to die?" **NUMBERS 17:10-13**

Ways I might respond to grumbling that encourage godliness instead:

My prayer for genuine spiritual life and health to put an end to grumbling in our home:

Other prayer concerns today:

March 13

NUMBERS 19:1–20:29
LUKE 1:1-25
PSALM 56:1-13
PROVERBS 11:8

Don't be afraid, Zechariah! God has heard your prayer. Your wife, Elizabeth, will give you a son, and you are to name him John. You will have great joy and gladness, and many will rejoice at his birth, for he will be great in the eyes of the Lord. He must never touch wine or other alcoholic drinks. He will be filled with the Holy Spirit, even before his birth. And he will turn many Israelites to the Lord their God. He will be a man with the spirit and power of Elijah. He will prepare the people for the coming of the Lord. He will turn the hearts of the fathers to their children, and he will cause those who are rebellious to accept the wisdom of the godly. **LUKE 1:13-17**

Ways our hearts and the hearts of our children need to turn toward one another:

My prayer for the Lord to work in my heart to respond to my children with grace and mercy:

Other prayer concerns today:

March 14

NUMBERS 21:1–22:20
LUKE 1:26-56
PSALM 57:1-11
PROVERBS 11:9-11

The LORD sent poisonous snakes among the people, and many were bitten and died. Then the people came to Moses and cried out, "We have sinned by speaking against the LORD and against you. Pray that the LORD will take away the snakes." So Moses prayed for the people. Then the LORD told him, "Make a replica of a poisonous snake and attach it to a pole. All who are bitten will live if they simply look at it!" So Moses made a snake out of bronze and attached it to a pole. Then anyone who was bitten by a snake could look at the bronze snake and be healed! **NUMBERS 21:6-9**

Ways I long for my child to find life and healing by looking to Jesus:

My prayer for my child to look to Jesus' finished work on the cross to find life:

Other prayer concerns today:

March 15

NUMBERS 22:21–23:30
LUKE 1:57-80
PSALM 58:1-11
PROVERBS 11:12-13

It is foolish to belittle one's neighbor;
a sensible person keeps quiet.
A gossip goes around telling secrets,
but those who are trustworthy can keep a confidence.

PROVERBS 11:12-13

Things my child may have overheard me talk about in the last week:

My prayer to grow in keeping the confidences of others:

Other prayer concerns today:

March 16

NUMBERS 24:1–25:18
LUKE 2:1-35
PSALM 59:1-17
PROVERBS 11:14

Jesus' parents were amazed at what was being said about him. Then Simeon blessed them, and he said to Mary, the baby's mother, "This child is destined to cause many in Israel to fall, and many others to rise. He has been sent as a sign from God, but many will oppose him. As a result, the deepest thoughts of many hearts will be revealed. And a sword will pierce your very soul." **LUKE 2:33-35**

Aspects of my child's life I want to trust Christ with, even though they bring pain:

My prayer that Jesus will be a joy to my child:

Other prayer concerns today:

March 17

NUMBERS 26:1-51
LUKE 2:36-52
PSALM 60:1-12
PROVERBS 11:15

Jesus grew in wisdom and in stature
and in favor with God and all the people.
LUKE 2:52

Ways I long for my child to grow in wisdom, in stature, and in favor with God and others:

My prayer for wisdom to parent my child toward growth in wisdom, stature, and favor:

Other prayer concerns today:

March 18

NUMBERS 26:52–28:15
LUKE 3:1-22
PSALM 61:1-8
PROVERBS 11:16-17

One day a petition was presented by the daughters of Zelophehad—Mahlah, Noah, Hoglah, Milcah, and Tirzah. Their father, Zelophehad, was a descendant of Hepher son of Gilead, son of Makir, son of Manasseh, son of Joseph. These women stood before Moses, Eleazar the priest, the tribal leaders, and the entire community at the entrance of the Tabernacle. "Our father died in the wilderness," they said. "He was not among Korah's followers, who rebelled against the LORD; he died because of his own sin. But he had no sons. Why should the name of our father disappear from his clan just because he had no sons? Give us property along with the rest of our relatives." **NUMBERS 27:1-4**

Promises of God I want my child to boldly desire:

My prayer for my child to inherit everything God has promised:

Other prayer concerns today:

March 19

NUMBERS 28:16–29:40
LUKE 3:23-38
PSALM 62:1-12
PROVERBS 11:18-19

One day when the crowds were being baptized, Jesus himself was baptized. As he was praying, the heavens opened, and the Holy Spirit, in bodily form, descended on him like a dove. And a voice from heaven said, "You are my dearly loved Son, and you bring me great joy." Jesus was about thirty years old when he began his public ministry. Jesus was known as the son of Joseph. Joseph was the son of Heli. . . . Seth was the son of Adam. Adam was the son of God. **LUKE 3:21-23, 38**

Ways I'm so grateful my child pleases us and ways I hope he or she will please God:

My prayer of gratitude and rest in knowing that God is pleased with me because of my union with Christ:

Other prayer concerns today:

March 20

NUMBERS 30:1–31:54
LUKE 4:1-30
PSALM 63:1-11
PROVERBS 11:20-21

Moses summoned the leaders of the tribes of Israel and told them, "This is what the LORD has commanded: A man who makes a vow to the LORD or makes a pledge under oath must never break it. He must do exactly what he said he would do." **NUMBERS 30:1-2**

Commitments I want my child to see me fulfill:

My prayer for the Spirit to work his faithfulness into the fabric of our family:

Other prayer concerns today:

March 21

NUMBERS 32:1–33:39
LUKE 4:31–5:11
PSALM 64:1-10
PROVERBS 11:22

This is the route the Israelites followed as they marched out of Egypt under the leadership of Moses and Aaron. At the LORD*'s direction, Moses kept a written record of their progress. These are the stages of their march, identified by the different places where they stopped along the way.* **NUMBERS 33:1-2**

Significant markers in the life of our family where we've experienced grace:

My prayer for God to fill the ordinary days of our lives with his goodness:

Other prayer concerns today:

March 22

NUMBERS 33:40–35:34
LUKE 5:12-28
PSALM 65:1-13
PROVERBS 11:23

Later, as Jesus left the town, he saw a tax collector named Levi sitting at his tax collector's booth. "Follow me and be my disciple," Jesus said to him. So Levi got up, left everything, and followed him. **LUKE 5:27-28**

Transformation I long to see in my child:

My prayer for my child to get up, leave everything, and follow Jesus:

Other prayer concerns today:

March 23

NUMBERS 36:1–
DEUTERONOMY 1:46

LUKE 5:29–6:11

PSALM 66:1-20

PROVERBS 11:24-26

Jesus answered them, "Healthy people don't need a doctor—sick people do. I have come to call not those who think they are righteous, but those who know they are sinners and need to repent." **LUKE 5:31-32**

Changes I long to see in my heart and my child's heart:

My prayer for God to do the heart change in me and in my child that only he can do:

Other prayer concerns today:

March 24

DEUTERONOMY 2:1–3:29
LUKE 6:12-38
PSALM 67:1-7
PROVERBS 11:27

To you who are willing to listen, I say, love your enemies! Do good to those who hate you. Bless those who curse you. Pray for those who hurt you. If someone slaps you on one cheek, offer the other cheek also. If someone demands your coat, offer your shirt also. Give to anyone who asks; and when things are taken away from you, don't try to get them back. Do to others as you would like them to do to you. **LUKE 6:27-31**

People in our lives we need to pray for rather than avoid or resent:

My prayer for the spiritual power I need to love those who have hurt or offended me:

Other prayer concerns today:

March 25

DEUTERONOMY 4:1-49
LUKE 6:39–7:10
PSALM 68:1-18
PROVERBS 11:28

How can you think of saying, "Friend, let me help you get rid of that speck in your eye," when you can't see past the log in your own eye? Hypocrite! First get rid of the log in your own eye; then you will see well enough to deal with the speck in your friend's eye. **LUKE 6:42**

Sins I may be justifying or ignoring that I need to confess and forsake:

My prayer for the humility to confess and the power to forsake my own sins:

Other prayer concerns today:

March 26

DEUTERONOMY 5:1–6:25
LUKE 7:11-35
PSALM 68:19-35
PROVERBS 11:29-31

You must love the L*ORD your God with all your heart, all your soul, and all your strength. And you must commit yourselves wholeheartedly to these commands that I am giving you today. Repeat them again and again to your children. Talk about them when you are at home and when you are on the road, when you are going to bed and when you are getting up. Tie them to your hands and wear them on your forehead as reminders. Write them on the doorposts of your house and on your gates.* **DEUTERONOMY 6:5-9**

Times throughout our days when I could turn the conversation toward biblical truths:

My prayer that biblical truth and love for Jesus would shape my conversations with my child:

Other prayer concerns today:

DEUTERONOMY 7:1–8:20
LUKE 7:36–8:3
PSALM 69:1-18
PROVERBS 12:1

March 27

The LORD did not set his heart on you and choose you because you were more numerous than other nations, for you were the smallest of all nations! Rather, it was simply that the LORD loves you, and he was keeping the oath he had sworn to your ancestors. That is why the LORD rescued you with such a strong hand from your slavery and from the oppressive hand of Pharaoh, king of Egypt. **DEUTERONOMY 7:7-8**

Ways I can communicate my love for my child to my child:

My prayer of gratitude to God for choosing to set his love on me:

Other prayer concerns today:

March 28

DEUTERONOMY 9:1–10:22
LUKE 8:4-21
PSALM 69:19-36
PROVERBS 12:2-3

The seeds that fell on the good soil represent honest, good-hearted people who hear God's word, cling to it, and patiently produce a huge harvest. **LUKE 8:15**

Spiritual fruit I long to see in my child's life:

My prayer for a huge harvest of spiritual fruit in my life and my child's life:

Other prayer concerns today:

March 29

DEUTERONOMY 11:1–12:32
LUKE 8:22-39
PSALM 70:1-5
PROVERBS 12:4

The disciples were terrified and amazed. "Who is this man?" they asked each other. "When he gives a command, even the wind and waves obey him!" **LUKE 8:25**

Ways I long to see the power and authority of Jesus in our home:

My prayer for Jesus to exercise his power and authority to settle, purify, protect, and heal our family:

Other prayer concerns today:

March 30

DEUTERONOMY 13:1–15:23
LUKE 8:40–9:6
PSALM 71:1-24
PROVERBS 12:5-7

Suppose your servant says, "I will not leave you," because he loves you and your family, and he has done well with you. In that case, take an awl and push it through his earlobe into the door. After that, he will be your servant for life. And do the same for your female servants. **DEUTERONOMY 15:16-17**

Ways my life could better reflect that I am a bond-slave to Christ:

My prayer that my child center his or her identity on being a servant of Jesus:

Other prayer concerns today:

March 31

DEUTERONOMY 16:1–17:20
LUKE 9:7-27
PSALM 72:1-20
PROVERBS 12:8-9

"The Son of Man must suffer many terrible things," he said. "He will be rejected by the elders, the leading priests, and the teachers of religious law. He will be killed, but on the third day he will be raised from the dead." Then he said to the crowd, "If any of you wants to be my follower, you must give up your own way, take up your cross daily, and follow me." **LUKE 9:22-23**

Hardships I'm praying will be used in my child's life to form character:

My prayer for our family to follow Christ, even when it is costly:

Other prayer concerns today:

April 1

DEUTERONOMY 18:1–20:20
LUKE 9:28-50
PSALM 73:1-28
PROVERBS 12:10

I tried to understand why the wicked prosper.
But what a difficult task it is!
Then I went into your sanctuary, O God,
and I finally understood the destiny of the wicked.
PSALM 73:16-17

Questions my child may have now or in the future that I can trust God to work through:

My prayer that my child will take seriously the ruin that awaits those who reject God and the glory that awaits those who desire him:

Other prayer concerns today:

April 2

DEUTERONOMY 21:1–22:30
LUKE 9:51–10:12
PSALM 74:1-23
PROVERBS 12:11

Suppose a man has a stubborn and rebellious son who will not obey his father or mother, even though they discipline him. . . . Purge this evil from among you, and all Israel will hear about it. **DEUTERONOMY 21:18, 21**

Areas in which I pray for greater obedience in my child:

My prayer of gratitude for God's firstborn, whose death for our rebellion has changed the trajectory of our family's future:

Other prayer concerns today:

April 3

Don't rejoice because evil spirits obey you; rejoice because your names are registered in heaven. . . . No one truly knows the Son except the Father, and no one truly knows the Father except the Son and those to whom the Son chooses to reveal him. **LUKE 10:20, 22**

DEUTERONOMY 23:1–25:19
LUKE 10:13-37
PSALM 75:1-10
PROVERBS 12:12-14

A list of names I pray are registered in heaven:

My prayer for Jesus to reveal himself to all these loved ones:

Other prayer concerns today:

April 4

DEUTERONOMY 26:1–27:26
LUKE 10:38–11:13
PSALM 76:1-12
PROVERBS 12:15-17

You fathers—if your children ask for a fish, do you give them a snake instead? Or if they ask for an egg, do you give them a scorpion? Of course not! So if you sinful people know how to give good gifts to your children, how much more will your heavenly Father give the Holy Spirit to those who ask him. **LUKE 11:11-13**

Good things I pray the Father will give to my child:

My prayer for God to give my child the good gift of the Holy Spirit:

Other prayer concerns today:

April 5

DEUTERONOMY 28:1-68
LUKE 11:14-36
PSALM 77:1-20
PROVERBS 12:18

You will experience all these blessings
if you obey the LORD your God:

Your towns and your fields
will be blessed.
Your children and your crops
will be blessed. . . .
Wherever you go and whatever you do,
you will be blessed.
DEUTERONOMY 28:2-4, 6

Ways I pray the Lord will bless our children:

My prayer of gratitude for the complete obedience of Christ that makes it possible for the Lord to bless us even though we've disobeyed:

Other prayer concerns today:

DEUTERONOMY 29:1–30:20
LUKE 11:37–12:7
PSALM 78:1-31
PROVERBS 12:19-20

April 6

When you experience all these blessings and curses I have listed for you, and when you are living among the nations to which the L*ORD your God has exiled you, take to heart all these instructions. If at that time you and your children return to the* L*ORD your God, and if you obey with all your heart and all your soul all the commands I have given you today, then the* L*ORD your God will restore your fortunes. He will have mercy on you and gather you back from all the nations where he has scattered you. . . . The* L*ORD your God will change your heart and the hearts of all your descendants, so that you will love him with all your heart and soul and so you may live!* **DEUTERONOMY 30:1-3, 6**

Implications of the truth that I am powerless to generate spiritual life in myself or my child:

My prayer of welcome for the Spirit to change my heart and the heart of my child so we will love the Lord completely:

Other prayer concerns today:

April 7

DEUTERONOMY 31:1–32:27
LUKE 12:8-34
PSALM 78:32-55
PROVERBS 12:21-23

Can all your worries add a single moment to your life? And if worry can't accomplish a little thing like that, what's the use of worrying over bigger things? **LUKE 12:25-26**

Implications of having a Father who knows all our needs:

My prayer of confession over my tendency to worry rather than trust God:

Other prayer concerns today:

DEUTERONOMY 32:28-52
LUKE 12:35-59
PSALM 78:56-64
PROVERBS 12:24

April 8

When Moses had finished reciting all these words to the people of Israel, he added: "Take to heart all the words of warning I have given you today. Pass them on as a command to your children so they will obey every word of these instructions. These instructions are not empty words—they are your life! By obeying them you will enjoy a long life in the land you will occupy when you cross the Jordan River." **DEUTERONOMY 32:45-47**

Words I want to say more and words I want to say less in our home:

My prayer for my words to be life-giving to my child:

Other prayer concerns today:

April 9

DEUTERONOMY 33:1-29
LUKE 13:1-21
PSALM 78:65-72
PROVERBS 12:25

Jesus said, "What is the Kingdom of God like? How can I illustrate it? It is like a tiny mustard seed that a man planted in a garden; it grows and becomes a tree, and the birds make nests in its branches." He also asked, "What else is the Kingdom of God like? It is like the yeast a woman used in making bread. Even though she put only a little yeast in three measures of flour, it permeated every part of the dough." **LUKE 13:18-21**

Growth I long to see in my child's life:

My prayer for spiritual growth in my life and my child's life:

Other prayer concerns today:

April 10

DEUTERONOMY 34:1–JOSHUA 2:24
LUKE 13:22–14:6
PSALM 79:1-13
PROVERBS 12:26

O Jerusalem, Jerusalem, the city that kills the prophets and stones God's messengers! How often I have wanted to gather your children together as a hen protects her chicks beneath her wings, but you wouldn't let me. **LUKE 13:34**

Limits to the protection I can provide to my child:

My prayer for my child to be protected by Christ from ultimate harm:

Other prayer concerns today:

April 11

JOSHUA 3:1–4:24
LUKE 14:7-35
PSALM 80:1-19
PROVERBS 12:27-28

Joshua said to the Israelites, "In the future your children will ask, 'What do these stones mean?' Then you can tell them, 'This is where the Israelites crossed the Jordan on dry ground.' For the LORD your God dried up the river right before your eyes, and he kept it dry until you were all across, just as he did at the Red Sea when he dried it up until we had all crossed over. He did this so all the nations of the earth might know that the LORD's hand is powerful, and so you might fear the LORD your God forever." **JOSHUA 4:21-24**

What I need to do to make sure my child understands what it means to partake in Communion, the memorial meal to Christ's death and resurrection:

My prayer that the Spirit will infuse the memorial sign of Communion with meaning in our family's life:

Other prayer concerns today:

April 12

JOSHUA 5:1–7:15
LUKE 15:1-32
PSALM 81:1-16
PROVERBS 13:1

His father said to him, "Look, dear son, you have always stayed by me, and everything I have is yours. We had to celebrate this happy day. For your brother was dead and has come back to life! He was lost, but now he is found!" **LUKE 15:31-32**

Ways my child needs a more profound grasp of the gospel:

My prayer for those seeking satisfaction away from Christ and those who have confused good behavior with being in close relationship to him:

Other prayer concerns today:

April 13

JOSHUA 7:16–9:2
LUKE 16:1-18
PSALM 82:1-8
PROVERBS 13:2-3

Joshua said to Achan, "Why have you brought trouble on us? The LORD will now bring trouble on you." **JOSHUA 7:25**

Ways I long for our troubles to be transformed by grace and mercy:

My prayer for our family to be a display of God's grace and mercy:

Other prayer concerns today:

April 14

JOSHUA 9:3–10:43
LUKE 16:19–17:10
PSALM 83:1-18
PROVERBS 13:4

"If another believer sins, rebuke that person; then if there is repentance, forgive. Even if that person wrongs you seven times a day and each time turns again and asks forgiveness, you must forgive." The apostles said to the Lord, "Show us how to increase our faith." The Lord answered, "If you had faith even as small as a mustard seed, you could say to this mulberry tree, 'May you be uprooted and be planted in the sea,' and it would obey you!" **LUKE 17:3-6**

People I need to forgive:

My prayer for faith to surrender the deep hurts in my life to God:

Other prayer concerns today:

April 15

JOSHUA 11:1–12:24
LUKE 17:11-37
PSALM 84:1-12
PROVERBS 13:5-6

How lovely is your dwelling place,
O LORD of Heaven's Armies.
I long, yes, I faint with longing
to enter the courts of the LORD.
With my whole being, body and soul,
I will shout joyfully to the living God.
PSALM 84:1-2

Reasons to long for close fellowship with God through Christ:

My prayer for my child to be homesick for God:

Other prayer concerns today:

April 16

JOSHUA 13:1–14:15
LUKE 18:1-17
PSALM 85:1-13
PROVERBS 13:7-8

The tax collector stood at a distance and dared not even lift his eyes to heaven as he prayed. Instead, he beat his chest in sorrow, saying, "O God, be merciful to me, for I am a sinner." I tell you, this sinner, not the Pharisee, returned home justified before God. For those who exalt themselves will be humbled, and those who humble themselves will be exalted. **LUKE 18:13-14**

The last specific sin I can remember confessing:

My prayer for the humility to be honest about my own sin struggles:

Other prayer concerns today:

April 17

JOSHUA 15:1-63
LUKE 18:18-43
PSALM 86:1-17
PROVERBS 13:9-10

When Jesus saw this, he said, "How hard it is for the rich to enter the Kingdom of God! In fact, it is easier for a camel to go through the eye of a needle than for a rich person to enter the Kingdom of God!" Those who heard this said, "Then who in the world can be saved?" He replied, "What is impossible for people is possible with God." **LUKE 18:24-27**

Evidences of spiritual life that are impossible for me to generate in my child's life:

My prayer for God to do what I cannot do in my child's life:

Other prayer concerns today:

April 18

JOSHUA 16:1–18:28
LUKE 19:1-27
PSALM 87:1-7
PROVERBS 13:11

Jesus responded, "Salvation has come to this home today, for this man has shown himself to be a true son of Abraham. For the Son of Man came to seek and save those who are lost." **LUKE 19:9-10**

Ways I want the generosity of God's grace in my life to make me generous with grace:

My prayer for growing in gracious generosity:

Other prayer concerns today:

April 19

JOSHUA 19:1–20:9
LUKE 19:28-48
PSALM 88:1-18
PROVERBS 13:12-14

O Lord, God of my salvation,
I cry out to you by day.
I come to you at night.
Now hear my prayer;
listen to my cry.
For my life is full of troubles,
and death draws near.
I am as good as dead,
like a strong man with no strength left.
PSALM 88:1-4

Troubles that tempt me to despair:

My prayer to the God of my salvation for deliverance from hopelessness:

Other prayer concerns today:

April 20

JOSHUA 21:1–22:20
LUKE 20:1-26
PSALM 89:1-13
PROVERBS 13:15-16

The Lord gave to Israel all the land he had sworn to give their ancestors, and they took possession of it and settled there. And the Lord gave them rest on every side, just as he had solemnly promised their ancestors. None of their enemies could stand against them, for the Lord helped them conquer all their enemies. Not a single one of all the good promises the Lord had given to the family of Israel was left unfulfilled; everything he had spoken came true. **JOSHUA 21:43-45**

Promises I'm counting on God fulfilling:

My prayer for my child to see beyond this life to the blessings of the next:

Other prayer concerns today:

April 21

JOSHUA 22:21–23:16
LUKE 20:27-47
PSALM 89:14-37
PROVERBS 13:17-19

If you turn away from him and cling to the customs of the survivors of these nations remaining among you, and if you intermarry with them, then know for certain that the LORD your God will no longer drive them out of your land. Instead, they will be a snare and a trap to you, a whip for your backs and thorny brambles in your eyes, and you will vanish from this good land the LORD your God has given you. **JOSHUA 23:12-13**

How I want to respond when my child makes unwise choices in matters of the heart:

My prayer for my child to avoid the misery of being unequally yoked to an unbeliever:

Other prayer concerns today:

April 22

JOSHUA 24:1-33
LUKE 21:1-28
PSALM 89:38-52
PROVERBS 13:20-23

Fear the LORD and serve him wholeheartedly. Put away forever the idols your ancestors worshiped when they lived beyond the Euphrates River and in Egypt. Serve the LORD alone. But if you refuse to serve the LORD, then choose today whom you will serve. Would you prefer the gods your ancestors served beyond the Euphrates? Or will it be the gods of the Amorites in whose land you now live? But as for me and my family, we will serve the LORD. **JOSHUA 24:14-15**

Idols that have been hard to eradicate from our home and our hearts:

My prayer of determination to serve the Lord:

Other prayer concerns today:

April 23

JUDGES 1:1–2:9
LUKE 21:29–22:13
PSALMS 90:1–91:16
PROVERBS 13:24-25

Lord, through all the generations
you have been our home! . . .
Satisfy us each morning with your unfailing love,
so we may sing for joy to the end of our lives.
Give us gladness in proportion to our former misery!
Replace the evil years with good.
Let us, your servants, see you work again;
let our children see your glory.
PSALM 90:1, 14-16

Ways we long to see God at work in our family:

My prayer for my child to see the glory of God and be drawn to it:

Other prayer concerns today:

April 24

JUDGES 2:10–3:31
LUKE 22:14-34
PSALMS 92:1–93:5
PROVERBS 14:1-2

After that generation died, another generation grew up who did not acknowledge the LORD or remember the mighty things he had done for Israel. The Israelites did evil in the LORD's sight and served the images of Baal. They abandoned the LORD, the God of their ancestors, who had brought them out of Egypt. They went after other gods, worshiping the gods of the people around them. And they angered the LORD. **JUDGES 2:10-12**

My part in passing along a living faith to my child:

My prayer for my child to experience what it means to trust God to deliver his promised help:

Other prayer concerns today:

April 25

JUDGES 4:1–5:31
LUKE 22:35-53
PSALM 94:1-23
PROVERBS 14:3-4

They crush your people, LORD,
hurting those you claim as your own.
They kill widows and foreigners
and murder orphans.
"The LORD isn't looking," they say,
"and besides, the God of Israel doesn't care."
Think again, you fools!
PSALM 94:5-8

Hurts I must entrust to the Lord's timing, the Lord's ways, and his perfect justice:

My prayer for the grace to wait for the Lord to set things right:

Other prayer concerns today:

April 26

JUDGES 6:1-40
LUKE 22:54–23:12
PSALMS 95:1–96:13
PROVERBS 14:5-6

The LORD turned to him and said, "Go with the strength you have, and rescue Israel from the Midianites. I am sending you!" "But Lord," Gideon replied, "how can I rescue Israel? My clan is the weakest in the whole tribe of Manasseh, and I am the least in my entire family!" The LORD said to him, "I will be with you. And you will destroy the Midianites as if you were fighting against one man." **JUDGES 6:14-16**

Situations in which I can trust that God will be with me and my child:

My prayer for the power of God to be put on display in my child's weakness:

Other prayer concerns today:

April 27

JUDGES 7:1–8:17
LUKE 23:13-43
PSALMS 97:1–98:9
PROVERBS 14:7-8

One of the criminals hanging beside him scoffed, "So you're the Messiah, are you? Prove it by saving yourself—and us, too, while you're at it!" But the other criminal protested, "Don't you fear God even when you have been sentenced to die? We deserve to die for our crimes, but this man hasn't done anything wrong." Then he said, "Jesus, remember me when you come into your Kingdom." And Jesus replied, "I assure you, today you will be with me in paradise." **LUKE 23:39-43**

People in my life who have so far resisted calling out to Christ for salvation:

My prayer for loved ones to come to the end of their rejection of Christ:

Other prayer concerns today:

April 28

JUDGES 8:18–9:21
LUKE 23:44–24:12
PSALM 99:1-9
PROVERBS 14:9-10

The Israelites said to Gideon, "Be our ruler! You and your son and your grandson will be our rulers, for you have rescued us from Midian." But Gideon replied, "I will not rule over you, nor will my son. The Lord *will rule over you! However, I do have one request—that each of you give me an earring from the plunder you collected from your fallen enemies."* **JUDGES 8:22-24**

Leaders who have lived in integrity and faithfulness before me and my child for which I'm grateful:

My prayer for Christian leaders who have influence in my child's life:

Other prayer concerns today:

April 29

JUDGES 9:22–10:18
LUKE 24:13-53
PSALM 100:1-5
PROVERBS 14:11-12

And [Jesus] said, "Yes, it was written long ago that the Messiah would suffer and die and rise from the dead on the third day. It was also written that this message would be proclaimed in the authority of his name to all the nations, beginning in Jerusalem: 'There is forgiveness of sins for all who repent.'" **LUKE 24:46-47**

What my child might say is the gospel according to our family:

My prayer for words and ways to show that we value repentance and forgiveness in our home:

Other prayer concerns today:

April 30

JUDGES 11:1–12:15
JOHN 1:1-28
PSALM 101:1-8
PROVERBS 14:13-14

He came into the very world he created, but the world didn't recognize him. He came to his own people, and even they rejected him. But to all who believed him and accepted him, he gave the right to become children of God. They are reborn—not with a physical birth resulting from human passion or plan, but a birth that comes from God. **JOHN 1:10-13**

Signs of spiritual life I long to see in my child:

My prayer for God to give my child the spiritual life and health only he can provide:

Other prayer concerns today:

May 1

JUDGES 13:1–14:20
JOHN 1:29-51
PSALM 102:1-28
PROVERBS 14:15-16

His father and mother objected. "Isn't there even one woman in our tribe or among all the Israelites you could marry?" they asked. "Why must you go to the pagan Philistines to find a wife?" But Samson told his father, "Get her for me! She looks good to me." His father and mother didn't realize the LORD *was at work in this, creating an opportunity to work against the Philistines, who ruled over Israel at that time.* **JUDGES 14:3-4**

Times in my life when God was at work in ways I couldn't see:

My prayer for God to cause even my child's foolish choices to work together for good:

Other prayer concerns today:

May 2

JUDGES 15:1–16:31
JOHN 2:1-25
PSALM 103:1-22
PROVERBS 14:17-19

The LORD is like a father to his children,
tender and compassionate to those who fear him.
For he knows how weak we are;
he remembers we are only dust.
PSALM 103:13-14

Regrets I need the Lord's tenderness to help me let go of:

My prayer to receive compassion from my heavenly Father so I can release my failures and regrets:

Other prayer concerns today:

May 3

JUDGES 17:1–18:31
JOHN 3:1-21
PSALM 104:1-23
PROVERBS 14:20-21

Jesus replied, "I assure you, no one can enter the Kingdom of God without being born of water and the Spirit. Humans can reproduce only human life, but the Holy Spirit gives birth to spiritual life. So don't be surprised when I say, 'You must be born again.' The wind blows wherever it wants. Just as you can hear the wind but can't tell where it comes from or where it is going, so you can't explain how people are born of the Spirit." **JOHN 3:5-8**

Admission of my inability to generate spiritual life in myself and my child:

My prayer for the Spirit to generate the spiritual life I long for:

Other prayer concerns today:

JUDGES 19:1–20:48
JOHN 3:22–4:3
PSALM 104:24-35
PROVERBS 14:22-24

May 4

He must become greater and greater,
and I must become less and less.
JOHN 3:30

Ways I can encourage my child to make much of Christ rather than self:

My prayer to know when to affirm and celebrate my child, and when to point out pride and self-centeredness:

Other prayer concerns today:

May 5

JUDGES 21:1—RUTH 1:22
JOHN 4:4-42
PSALM 105:1-15
PROVERBS 14:25

In the days when the judges ruled in Israel, a severe famine came upon the land. So a man from Bethlehem in Judah left his home and went to live in the country of Moab, taking his wife and two sons with him. The man's name was Elimelech, and his wife was Naomi. Their two sons were Mahlon and Kilion. They were Ephrathites from Bethlehem in the land of Judah. And when they reached Moab, they settled there. **RUTH 1:1-2**

Ways I can foster a pilgrim lifestyle in our home:

My prayer to live in this world like the citizen of another:

Other prayer concerns today:

May 6

RUTH 2:1–4:22
JOHN 4:43-54
PSALM 105:16-36
PROVERBS 14:26-27

The women of the town said to Naomi, "Praise the L*ORD, who has now provided a redeemer for your family! May this child be famous in Israel. May he restore your youth and care for you in your old age. For he is the son of your daughter-in-law who loves you and has been better to you than seven sons!"* **RUTH 4:14-15**

What I've considered to be the "perfect family":

My prayer of faith that God intends to work in and through my less-than-perfect family:

Other prayer concerns today:

May 7

1 SAMUEL 1:1–2:21
JOHN 5:1-23
PSALM 105:37-45
PROVERBS 14:28-29

The sons of Eli were worthless men. They did not know the L*ORD. The custom of the priests with the people was that when any man offered sacrifice, the priest's servant would come, while the meat was boiling, with a three-pronged fork in his hand, and he would thrust it into the pan or kettle or cauldron or pot. All that the fork brought up the priest would take for himself. . . . Now Eli was very old, and he kept hearing all that his sons were doing to all Israel, and how they lay with the women who were serving at the entrance to the tent of meeting.* **1 SAMUEL 2:12-14, 22, ESV**

Signs that I might fear the wrath or rejection of my child more than I fear God:

A prayer for courage to confront sin and do what is right to restrain it:

Other prayer concerns today:

May 8

1 SAMUEL 2:22–4:22
JOHN 5:24-47
PSALM 106:1-12
PROVERBS 14:30-31

Now in those days messages from the LORD were very rare, and visions were quite uncommon. One night Eli, who was almost blind by now, had gone to bed. The lamp of God had not yet gone out, and Samuel was sleeping in the Tabernacle near the Ark of God. Suddenly the LORD called out, "Samuel!" . . . Samuel did not yet know the LORD because he had never had a message from the LORD before. **1 SAMUEL 3:1-4, 7**

Specific Scriptures I long for my child to hear as from the Lord:

My prayer for my child to hear God speaking through his Word:

Other prayer concerns today:

May 9

1 SAMUEL 5:1–7:17
JOHN 6:1-21
PSALM 106:13-31
PROVERBS 14:32-33

After the Philistines captured the Ark of God, they took it from the battleground at Ebenezer to the town of Ashdod. They carried the Ark of God into the temple of Dagon and placed it beside an idol of Dagon. But when the citizens of Ashdod went to see it the next morning, Dagon had fallen with his face to the ground in front of the Ark of the LORD! So they took Dagon and put him in his place again. **1 SAMUEL 5:1-3**

Idols that need to be exposed as powerless to deliver what they promise:

My prayer for the spiritual strength to keep up the battle against idolatry:

Other prayer concerns today:

May 10

1 SAMUEL 8:1–9:27
JOHN 6:22-42
PSALM 106:32-48
PROVERBS 14:34-35

Jesus replied, "I am the bread of life. Whoever comes to me will never be hungry again. Whoever believes in me will never be thirsty. But you haven't believed in me even though you have seen me. However, those the Father has given me will come to me, and I will never reject them." **JOHN 6:35-37**

My statement of personal trust in the words of Jesus: "Those the Father has given me will come to me":

My prayer for my child to come to Christ:

Other prayer concerns today:

May 11

1 SAMUEL 10:1–11:15
JOHN 6:43-71
PSALM 107:1-43
PROVERBS 15:1-3

Jesus said again, "I tell you the truth, unless you eat the flesh of the Son of Man and drink his blood, you cannot have eternal life within you. But anyone who eats my flesh and drinks my blood has eternal life, and I will raise that person at the last day. For my flesh is true food, and my blood is true drink. Anyone who eats my flesh and drinks my blood remains in me, and I in him. I live because of the living Father who sent me; in the same way, anyone who feeds on me will live because of me." **JOHN 6:53-57**

The miracle that would take care of what I see as our most pressing problem today:

My prayer of gratitude that Jesus has met our most pressing problem by giving himself:

Other prayer concerns today:

May 12

1 SAMUEL 12:1–13:23
JOHN 7:1-30
PSALM 108:1-13
PROVERBS 15:4

Jesus traveled around Galilee. He wanted to stay out of Judea, where the Jewish leaders were plotting his death. But soon it was time for the Jewish Festival of Shelters, and Jesus' brothers said to him, "Leave here and go to Judea, where your followers can see your miracles! You can't become famous if you hide like this! If you can do such wonderful things, show yourself to the world!" For even his brothers didn't believe in him. **JOHN 7:1-5**

How it helps me to know that my child's salvation is not dependent on the perfection of my witness:

My prayer that long-term resistance to Christ will give way to a glad embrace of him:

Other prayer concerns today:

May 13

1 SAMUEL 14:1-52
JOHN 7:31-53
PSALM 109:1-31
PROVERBS 15:5-7

The men of Israel were pressed to exhaustion that day, because Saul had placed them under an oath, saying, "Let a curse fall on anyone who eats before evening—before I have full revenge on my enemies." . . . But Jonathan had not heard his father's command, and he dipped the end of his stick into a piece of honeycomb and ate the honey. **1 SAMUEL 14:24, 27**

Ways I might be tempted to try to look more spiritual than I really am:

My prayer to refuse to settle for merely appearing to be spiritual to others:

Other prayer concerns today:

May 14

1 SAMUEL 15:1–16:23
JOHN 8:1-20
PSALM 110:1-7
PROVERBS 15:8-10

The LORD said to Samuel, "Don't judge by his appearance or height, for I have rejected him. The LORD doesn't see things the way you see them. People judge by outward appearance, but the LORD looks at the heart." **1 SAMUEL 16:7**

My response to the reality that God can see into the reality of my heart:

My prayer for eyes to see people the way God does:

Other prayer concerns today:

May 15

1 SAMUEL 17:1–18:4
JOHN 8:21-30
PSALM 111:1-10
PROVERBS 15:11

Goliath, a Philistine champion from Gath, came out of the Philistine ranks to face the forces of Israel. He was over nine feet tall! He wore a bronze helmet, and his bronze coat of mail weighed 125 pounds. . . . Goliath stood and shouted a taunt across to the Israelites. "Why are you all coming out to fight?" he called. "I am the Philistine champion, but you are only the servants of Saul. Choose one man to come down here and fight me! If he kills me, then we will be your slaves. But if I kill him, you will be our slaves!" **1 SAMUEL 17:4-5, 8-9**

Reasons not to despair over sins that threaten to enslave me or my child:

My prayer of gratitude for our champion, Jesus Christ, and the sin-defeating victory he has won:

Other prayer concerns today:

1 SAMUEL 18:5–19:24
JOHN 8:31-59
PSALM 112:1-10
PROVERBS 15:12-14

May 16

Praise the LORD!
How joyful are those who fear the LORD
and delight in obeying his commands. . . .
They do not fear bad news;
they confidently trust the LORD to care for them.
PSALM 112:1, 7

Bad news I often find myself fearing:

My prayer for greater fear of the Lord and less fear of bad news:

Other prayer concerns today:

May 17

1 SAMUEL 20:1–21:15
JOHN 9:1-41
PSALMS 113:1–114:8
PROVERBS 15:15-17

As Jesus was walking along, he saw a man who had been blind from birth. "Rabbi," his disciples asked him, "why was this man born blind? Was it because of his own sins or his parents' sins?" "It was not because of his sins or his parents' sins," Jesus answered. "This happened so the power of God could be seen in him." **JOHN 9:1-3**

Ways we long for the power of God to be evident in our lives:

My prayer for God to put his power on display in our lives in whatever way he sees fit:

Other prayer concerns today:

May 18

1 SAMUEL 22:1–23:29
JOHN 10:1-21
PSALM 115:1-18
PROVERBS 15:18-19

The one who enters through the gate is the shepherd of the sheep. The gatekeeper opens the gate for him, and the sheep recognize his voice and come to him. He calls his own sheep by name and leads them out. After he has gathered his own flock, he walks ahead of them, and they follow him because they know his voice. **JOHN 10:2-4**

Ways my child needs the care of his or her Good Shepherd:

My prayer for my child to hear and respond to the voice of the Good Shepherd:

Other prayer concerns today:

May 19

1 SAMUEL 24:1–25:44
JOHN 10:22-42
PSALM 116:1-19
PROVERBS 15:20-21

My sheep listen to my voice; I know them, and they follow me. I give them eternal life, and they will never perish. No one can snatch them away from me, for my Father has given them to me, and he is more powerful than anyone else. No one can snatch them from the Father's hand. The Father and I are one. **JOHN 10:27-30**

Things I sometimes fear might have the power to snatch my child from God's hand:

My prayer for my child to hear God's voice and follow him:

Other prayer concerns today:

May 20

1 SAMUEL 26:1–28:25
JOHN 11:1-54
PSALM 117:1-2
PROVERBS 15:22-23

Martha said to Jesus, "Lord, if only you had been here, my brother would not have died. But even now I know that God will give you whatever you ask." Jesus told her, "Your brother will rise again." "Yes," Martha said, "he will rise when everyone else rises, at the last day." Jesus told her, "I am the resurrection and the life. Anyone who believes in me will live, even after dying. Everyone who lives in me and believes in me will never ever die. Do you believe this, Martha?" **JOHN 11:21-26**

Ways we can talk about and respond to death that reflect genuine belief in resurrection life:

My prayer for our family to grieve the losses of this life as those who have resurrection hope:

Other prayer concerns today:

May 21

1 SAMUEL 29:1–31:13
JOHN 11:55–12:19
PSALM 118:1-18
PROVERBS 15:24-26

David was now in great danger because all his men were very bitter about losing their sons and daughters, and they began to talk of stoning him. But David found strength in the LORD his God. Then he said to Abiathar the priest, "Bring me the ephod!" So Abiathar brought it. Then David asked the LORD, "Should I chase after this band of raiders? Will I catch them?" And the LORD told him, "Yes, go after them. You will surely recover everything that was taken from you!" **1 SAMUEL 30:6-8**

Parenting challenges I need divine strength and divine wisdom to handle:

My prayer for God's power and wisdom to parent my child:

Other prayer concerns today:

May 22

2 SAMUEL 1:1–2:11
JOHN 12:20-50
PSALM 118:19-29
PROVERBS 15:27-28

Jesus replied, "Now the time has come for the Son of Man to enter into his glory. I tell you the truth, unless a kernel of wheat is planted in the soil and dies, it remains alone. But its death will produce many new kernels—a plentiful harvest of new lives. Those who love their life in this world will lose it. Those who care nothing for their life in this world will keep it for eternity." **JOHN 12:23-25**

Dreams and desires I'm being called to die to so that I can be fruitful for Christ's Kingdom:

My prayer for the grace to be willing to die to self even as I live for Christ:

Other prayer concerns today:

May 23

2 SAMUEL 2:12–3:39
JOHN 13:1-30
PSALM 119:1-16
PROVERBS 15:29-30

Jesus knew that the Father had given him authority over everything and that he had come from God and would return to God. So he got up from the table, took off his robe, wrapped a towel around his waist, and poured water into a basin. Then he began to wash the disciples' feet, drying them with the towel he had around him. **JOHN 13:3-5**

Things my child and I cannot do for ourselves that we desperately need Christ to do:

My prayer for the cleansing that only Christ can accomplish:

Other prayer concerns today:

May 24

2 SAMUEL 4:1–6:23
JOHN 13:31–14:14
PSALM 119:17-32
PROVERBS 15:31-32

Then all the tribes of Israel went to David at Hebron and told him, "We are your own flesh and blood. In the past, when Saul was our king, you were the one who really led the forces of Israel. And the LORD told you, 'You will be the shepherd of my people Israel. You will be Israel's leader.'" So there at Hebron, King David made a covenant before the LORD with all the elders of Israel. And they anointed him king of Israel. **2 SAMUEL 5:1-3**

What my child and I need to grasp about living under the authority of Jesus:

My prayer to find joy in submitting to Christ's authority:

Other prayer concerns today:

May 25

2 SAMUEL 7:1–8:18
JOHN 14:15-31
PSALM 119:33-48
PROVERBS 15:33

For when you die and are buried with your ancestors, I will raise up one of your descendants, your own offspring, and I will make his kingdom strong. . . . Your house and your kingdom will continue before me for all time, and your throne will be secure forever. **2 SAMUEL 7:12, 16**

Things I can't control:

My prayer for greater trust in God for the things I don't control but he does:

Other prayer concerns today:

May 26

2 SAMUEL 9:1–11:27
JOHN 15:1-27
PSALM 119:49-64
PROVERBS 16:1-3

Yes, I am the vine; you are the branches. Those who remain in me, and I in them, will produce much fruit. For apart from me you can do nothing. Anyone who does not remain in me is thrown away like a useless branch and withers. Such branches are gathered into a pile to be burned. But if you remain in me and my words remain in you, you may ask for anything you want, and it will be granted! **JOHN 15:5-7**

What it means for me to "remain in" Jesus:

My prayer asking Jesus to shape my wants with his Word:

Other prayer concerns today:

May 27

2 SAMUEL 12:1-31
JOHN 16:1-33
PSALM 119:65-80
PROVERBS 16:4-5

It is best for you that I go away, because if I don't, the Advocate won't come. If I do go away, then I will send him to you. And when he comes, he will convict the world of its sin, and of God's righteousness, and of the coming judgment. . . . When the Spirit of truth comes, he will guide you into all truth. **JOHN 16:7-8, 13**

Things I'm depending on the Holy Spirit to do for my child:

My prayer for the Spirit to bring forth life, light, and beauty in my child's life:

Other prayer concerns today:

2 SAMUEL 13:1-39
JOHN 17:1-26
PSALM 119:81-96
PROVERBS 16:6-7

May 28

David's son Absalom had a beautiful sister named Tamar. And Amnon, her half brother, . . . became so obsessed with Tamar that he became ill. . . . Since he was stronger than she was, he raped her. **2 SAMUEL 13:1-2, 14**

Sin patterns I don't want to pass along to my child:

My prayer for sin patterns to be broken in our family:

Other prayer concerns today:

May 29

2 SAMUEL 14:1–15:22
JOHN 18:1-24
PSALM 119:97-112
PROVERBS 16:8-9

We can make our plans,
but the LORD determines our steps.
PROVERBS 16:9

Plans I have for my child (that I might not have even identified before):

My prayer to surrender my plans and welcome God's plans:

Other prayer concerns today:

May 30

2 SAMUEL 15:23–16:23
JOHN 18:25–19:22
PSALM 119:113-128
PROVERBS 16:10-11

Meanwhile, as Simon Peter was standing by the fire warming himself, they asked him again, "You're not one of his disciples, are you?" He denied it, saying, "No, I am not." But one of the household slaves of the high priest, a relative of the man whose ear Peter had cut off, asked, "Didn't I see you out there in the olive grove with Jesus?" Again Peter denied it. And immediately a rooster crowed. **JOHN 18:25-27**

Past failures in parenting that don't have to characterize me going forward:

My prayer for God's grace in my life to define me more than my past failures:

Other prayer concerns today:

May 31

2 SAMUEL 17:1-29
JOHN 19:23-42
PSALM 119:129-152
PROVERBS 16:12-13

Standing near the cross were Jesus' mother, and his mother's sister, Mary (the wife of Clopas), and Mary Magdalene. When Jesus saw his mother standing there beside the disciple he loved, he said to her, "Dear woman, here is your son." And he said to this disciple, "Here is your mother." And from then on this disciple took her into his home. **JOHN 19:25-27**

Ways that parenting has brought pain:

My prayer to catch a glimpse of the glory of God at work in and through my suffering:

Other prayer concerns today:

June 1

2 SAMUEL 18:1–19:10
JOHN 20:1-31
PSALM 119:153-176
PROVERBS 16:14-15

The man from Ethiopia arrived and said, "I have good news for my lord the king. Today the L*ORD has rescued you from all those who rebelled against you." "What about young Absalom?" the king demanded. "Is he all right?" And the Ethiopian replied, "May all of your enemies, my lord the king, both now and in the future, share the fate of that young man!" The king was overcome with emotion. He went up to the room over the gateway and burst into tears. And as he went, he cried, "O my son Absalom! My son, my son Absalom! If only I had died instead of you! O Absalom, my son, my son."* **2 SAMUEL 18:31-33**

Areas of rebellion I pray will be overcome by the Spirit:

My prayer for the Spirit to transform rebellion and resistance into glad obedience:

Other prayer concerns today:

June 2

2 SAMUEL 19:11–20:13
JOHN 21:1-25
PSALM 120:1-7
PROVERBS 16:16-17

Peter turned around and saw behind them the disciple Jesus loved—the one who had leaned over to Jesus during supper and asked, "Lord, who will betray you?" Peter asked Jesus, "What about him, Lord?" Jesus replied, "If I want him to remain alive until I return, what is that to you? As for you, follow me." **JOHN 21:20-22**

Ways I'm often tempted to compare our family to other families:

My prayer to focus on following Jesus in the parenting task he has entrusted to me:

Other prayer concerns today:

2 SAMUEL 20:14–21:22
ACTS 1:1-26
PSALM 121:1-8
PROVERBS 16:18

June 3

I look up to the mountains—
does my help come from there?
My help comes from the LORD,
who made heaven and earth!
He will not let you stumble;
the one who watches over you will not slumber.
Indeed, he who watches over Israel
never slumbers or sleeps.

PSALM 121:1-4

Areas in which I am very aware of my need for God's promised help:

My prayer for help:

Other prayer concerns today:

June 4

2 SAMUEL 22:1–23:23
ACTS 2:1-47
PSALM 122:1-9
PROVERBS 16:19-20

"Let everyone in Israel know for certain that God has made this Jesus, whom you crucified, to be both Lord and Messiah!" Peter's words pierced their hearts, and they said to him and to the other apostles, "Brothers, what should we do?" Peter replied, "Each of you must repent of your sins and turn to God, and be baptized in the name of Jesus Christ for the forgiveness of your sins. Then you will receive the gift of the Holy Spirit. This promise is to you, to your children, and to those far away—all who have been called by the Lord our God." **ACTS 2:36-39**

God's promise to me and my children that I want to claim:

My prayer for God to draw my child to take hold of this promise through repentance and faith:

Other prayer concerns today:

June 5

2 SAMUEL 23:24–24:25
ACTS 3:1-26
PSALM 123:1-4
PROVERBS 16:21-23

David replied, "I have come to buy your threshing floor and to build an altar to the LORD there, so that he will stop the plague." "Take it, my lord the king, and use it as you wish," Araunah said to David. "Here are oxen for the burnt offering, and you can use the threshing boards and ox yokes for wood to build a fire on the altar. I will give it all to you, Your Majesty, and may the LORD your God accept your sacrifice." But the king replied to Araunah, "No, I insist on buying it, for I will not present burnt offerings to the LORD my God that have cost me nothing." **2 SAMUEL 24:21-24**

Ways God is using parenting to make me more like him:

My prayer for God to continue using parenting to sanctify me:

Other prayer concerns today:

June 6

1 KINGS 1:1-53
ACTS 4:1-37
PSALM 124:1-8
PROVERBS 16:24

Kind words are like honey—
sweet to the soul and healthy for the body.
PROVERBS 16:24

Words I often say to my child that I want to replace with more nourishing messages:

My prayer for God to use my words to bring joy and health to my child:

Other prayer concerns today:

June 7

1 KINGS 2:1–3:2
ACTS 5:1-42
PSALM 125:1-5
PROVERBS 16:25

Observe the requirements of the LORD your God, and follow all his ways. Keep the decrees, commands, regulations, and laws written in the Law of Moses so that you will be successful in all you do and wherever you go. If you do this, then the LORD will keep the promise he made to me. He told me, "If your descendants live as they should and follow me faithfully with all their heart and soul, one of them will always sit on the throne of Israel." **1 KINGS 2:3-4**

Ways in which I want to be loyal to King Jesus:

My prayer for the Lord to instill loyalty in me and to forgive me for past disloyalty:

Other prayer concerns today:

June 8

1 KINGS 3:3–4:34
ACTS 6:1-15
PSALM 126:1-6
PROVERBS 16:26-27

Restore our fortunes, LORD,
as streams renew the desert.
Those who plant in tears
will harvest with shouts of joy.
PSALM 126:4-5

The kind of harvest I pray will one day be reaped in my child's life:

My prayer for God to transform my tears into an abundant harvest of joy:

Other prayer concerns today:

1 KINGS 5:1–6:38
ACTS 7:1-29
PSALM 127:1-5
PROVERBS 16:28-30

June 9

Unless the LORD builds a house,
the work of the builders is wasted.
PSALM 127:1

Signs that I think it is up to me to generate spiritual life in my child:

My prayer for God to do his saving, securing, and building work in our home and hearts:

Other prayer concerns today:

June 10

1 KINGS 7:1-51
ACTS 7:30-50
PSALM 128:1-6
PROVERBS 16:31-33

Your wife will be like a fruitful grapevine,
flourishing within your home.
Your children will be like vigorous young olive trees
as they sit around your table.
That is the L*ORD's blessing*
for those who fear him.
PSALM 128:3-4

Ways I'd like my child to impact the world:

My prayer for my child to advance the Kingdom of God:

Other prayer concerns today:

June 11

1 KINGS 8:1-66
ACTS 7:51–8:13
PSALM 129:1-8
PROVERBS 17:1

You stubborn people! You are heathen at heart and deaf to the truth. Must you forever resist the Holy Spirit? That's what your ancestors did, and so do you! **ACTS 7:51**

Times my child encounters Christ in the Word each week:

My prayer for the Spirit to overcome any resistance in my child's life to his truth:

Other prayer concerns today:

June 12

1 KINGS 9:1–10:29
ACTS 8:14-40
PSALM 130:1-8
PROVERBS 17:2-3

Lord, if you kept a record of our sins,
who, O Lord, could ever survive?
But you offer forgiveness,
that we might learn to fear you.
PSALM 130:3-4

My experience of mercy from God:

My prayer to extend the forgiveness I've received to others:

Other prayer concerns today:

June 13

1 KINGS 11:1–12:19
ACTS 9:1-25
PSALM 131:1-3
PROVERBS 17:4-5

The LORD had clearly instructed the people of Israel, "You must not marry them, because they will turn your hearts to their gods." Yet Solomon insisted on loving them anyway. He had 700 wives of royal birth and 300 concubines. And in fact, they did turn his heart away from the LORD. **1 KINGS 11:2-3**

Wisdom I want to share with my child regarding matters of the heart:

My prayer for God to give my child a spouse to encourage him or her to love Christ more:

Other prayer concerns today:

June 14

1 KINGS 12:20–13:34
ACTS 9:26-43
PSALM 132:1-18
PROVERBS 17:6

Grandchildren are the crowning glory of the aged;
parents are the pride of their children.
PROVERBS 17:6

Ways my parents have brought me shame or honor:

My prayer that I will bring honor to my child:

Other prayer concerns today:

June 15

1 KINGS 14:1–15:24
ACTS 10:1-23
PSALM 133:1-3
PROVERBS 17:7-8

How wonderful and pleasant it is
when brothers live together in harmony!
For harmony is as precious as the anointing oil
that was poured over Aaron's head,
that ran down his beard
and onto the border of his robe.
Harmony is as refreshing as the dew from Mount Hermon
that falls on the mountains of Zion.
And there the LORD *has pronounced his blessing,*
even life everlasting.
PSALM 133

Ways I'm modeling the joy and benefits of a life connected to the body of Christ:

My prayer that my child will find the good life among those who love Jesus:

Other prayer concerns today:

June 16

1 KINGS 15:25–17:24
ACTS 10:24-48
PSALM 134:1-3
PROVERBS 17:9-11

God shows no favoritism. In every nation he accepts those who fear him and do what is right. This is the message of Good News for the people of Israel—that there is peace with God through Jesus Christ, who is Lord of all. . . . Everyone who believes in him will have their sins forgiven through his name. **ACTS 10:34-36, 43**

Privileges our family has had that we don't want to take for granted:

My prayer for protection of my child from presumption and complacency:

Other prayer concerns today:

June 17

1 KINGS 18:1-46
ACTS 11:1-30
PSALM 135:1-21
PROVERBS 17:12-13

Then Elijah stood in front of them and said, "How much longer will you waver, hobbling between two opinions? If the L*ORD is God, follow him! But if Baal is God, then follow him!" But the people were completely silent.* **1 KINGS 18:21**

Signs that my child might be wavering between living for Christ and loving the world:

My prayer that following Christ will be the settled and singular aim of my child's life:

Other prayer concerns today:

June 18

1 KINGS 19:1-21
ACTS 12:1-23
PSALM 136:1-26
PROVERBS 17:14-15

He remembered us in our weakness.
His faithful love endures forever.
He saved us from our enemies.
His faithful love endures forever.
He gives food to every living thing.
His faithful love endures forever.
Give thanks to the God of heaven.
His faithful love endures forever.
PSALM 136:23-26

Evidence of God's faithful love toward me:

My prayer for my child to recognize the myriad ways the Lord demonstrates faithful love:

Other prayer concerns today:

1 KINGS 20:1–21:29
ACTS 12:24–13:15
PSALM 137:1-9
PROVERBS 17:16

June 19

It is senseless to pay to educate a fool, since he has no heart for learning.
PROVERBS 17:16

Area in which I want my child to walk in wisdom:

My prayer for my child to be willing to invest in slow growth toward godly wisdom:

Other prayer concerns today:

June 20

1 KINGS 22:1-53
ACTS 13:16-41
PSALM 138:1-8
PROVERBS 17:17-18

Though I am surrounded by troubles,
you will protect me from the anger of my enemies.
You reach out your hand,
and the power of your right hand saves me.
The LORD will work out his plans for my life.
PSALM 138:7-8

Ways in which I long to see the power of God's right hand at work in our family:

My prayer for the strength of God's hand to save, protect, and guide:

Other prayer concerns today:

June 21

2 KINGS 1:1–2:25
ACTS 13:42–14:7
PSALM 139:1-24
PROVERBS 17:19-21

You made all the delicate, inner parts of my body
and knit me together in my mother's womb.
Thank you for making me so wonderfully complex!
Your workmanship is marvelous—how well I know it.
You watched me as I was being formed in utter seclusion,
as I was woven together in the dark of the womb.
You saw me before I was born.
Every day of my life was recorded in your book.
Every moment was laid out
before a single day had passed.

PSALM 139:13-16

Aspects of God's sovereignty in our lives that I struggle to accept:

My prayer to welcome God's sovereign purposes and plans for our family:

Other prayer concerns today:

June 22

2 KINGS 3:1–4:17
ACTS 14:8-28
PSALM 140:1-13
PROVERBS 17:22

Elisha said to her as she stood in the doorway, "Next year at this time you will be holding a son in your arms!" "No, my lord!" she cried. "O man of God, don't deceive me and get my hopes up like that." But sure enough, the woman soon became pregnant. And at that time the following year she had a son, just as Elisha had said. **2 KINGS 4:15-17**

Confession of my inability to breathe spiritual life into my child and my confidence that Jesus can:

My prayer for the Spirit's work to make my child warm to the truth of the gospel:

Other prayer concerns today:

June 23

2 KINGS 4:18–5:27
ACTS 15:1-35
PSALM 141:1-10
PROVERBS 17:23

This conversion of Gentiles is exactly what the prophets predicted. As it is written:

"Afterward I will return
and restore the fallen house of David.
I will rebuild its ruins
and restore it,
so that the rest of humanity might seek the Lord,
including the Gentiles—
all those I have called to be mine."

ACTS 15:15-17

Ways our family needs rebuilding and restoration:

My prayer for God to rebuild and restore as only he can:

Other prayer concerns today:

June 24

2 KINGS 6:1–7:20
ACTS 15:36–16:15
PSALM 142:1-7
PROVERBS 17:24-25

Foolish children bring grief to their father
and bitterness to the one who gave them birth.
PROVERBS 17:25

Godly parents I know who have ungodly children and godly people I know who had ungodly parents:

My prayer for the grace to neither take all the credit nor assume all the blame for my child's choices:

Other prayer concerns today:

June 25

2 KINGS 8:1–9:13
ACTS 16:16-40
PSALM 143:1-12
PROVERBS 17:26

The jailer called for lights and ran to the dungeon and fell down trembling before Paul and Silas. Then he brought them out and asked, "Sirs, what must I do to be saved?" They replied, "Believe in the Lord Jesus and you will be saved, along with everyone in your household." And they shared the word of the Lord with him and with all who lived in his household. Even at that hour of the night, the jailer cared for them and washed their wounds. Then he and everyone in his household were immediately baptized. He brought them into his house and set a meal before them, and he and his entire household rejoiced because they all believed in God. **ACTS 16:29-34**

Members of our family and extended family who may not yet have experienced salvation through Christ:

My prayer for our entire household and extended family to find salvation and security in Christ:

Other prayer concerns today:

June 26

2 KINGS 9:14–10:31
ACTS 17:1-34
PSALM 144:1-15
PROVERBS 17:27-28

May our sons flourish in their youth
like well-nurtured plants.
May our daughters be like graceful pillars,
carved to beautify a palace.
PSALM 144:12

Areas in which I want my child to flourish:

My prayer for my child to live out of the spiritual blessings of being united to Christ:

Other prayer concerns today:

June 27

2 KINGS 10:32–12:21
ACTS 18:1-22
PSALM 145:1-21
PROVERBS 18:1

Let each generation tell its children of your mighty acts;
let them proclaim your power.
I will meditate on your majestic, glorious splendor
and your wonderful miracles.
Your awe-inspiring deeds will be on every tongue;
I will proclaim your greatness.
Everyone will share the story of your wonderful goodness;
they will sing with joy about your righteousness.
PSALM 145:4-7

Ways God has worked in my life that I want to talk about with my child:

My prayer of praise to God:

Other prayer concerns today:

June 28

2 KINGS 13:1–14:29
ACTS 18:23–19:12
PSALM 146:1-10
PROVERBS 18:2-3

Elisha died and was buried. Groups of Moabite raiders used to invade the land each spring. Once when some Israelites were burying a man, they spied a band of these raiders. So they hastily threw the corpse into the tomb of Elisha and fled. But as soon as the body touched Elisha's bones, the dead man revived and jumped to his feet! **2 KINGS 13:20-21**

Reasons I can hope for resurrection life to become reality in my family:

My prayer for Christ's resurrection power to break into our family:

Other prayer concerns today:

June 29

2 KINGS 15:1–16:20
ACTS 19:13-41
PSALM 147:1-20
PROVERBS 18:4-5

King Ahaz then went to Damascus to meet with King Tiglath-pileser of Assyria. While he was there, he took special note of the altar. Then he sent a model of the altar to Uriah the priest, along with its design in full detail. Uriah followed the king's instructions and built an altar just like it, and it was ready before the king returned from Damascus. **2 KINGS 16:10-11**

Pressures facing me and my child to be conformed to the world:

My prayer for courage to be different from the world around us:

Other prayer concerns today:

June 30

2 KINGS 17:1–18:12
ACTS 20:1-38
PSALM 148:1-14
PROVERBS 18:6-7

This disaster came upon the people of Israel because they worshiped other gods. . . . They had followed the practices of the pagan nations the LORD had driven from the land ahead of them, as well as the practices the kings of Israel had introduced. . . . Because the LORD was very angry with Israel, he swept them away from his presence. **2 KINGS 17:7-8, 18**

Things I'm grateful to know make God angry:

My prayer for my child to find refuge from God's righteous anger by being joined to Christ:

Other prayer concerns today:

July 1

2 KINGS 18:13–19:37
ACTS 21:1-17
PSALM 149:1-9
PROVERBS 18:8

Then the Assyrian king's chief of staff told them to give this message to Hezekiah: "This is what the great king of Assyria says: What are you trusting in that makes you so confident? . . . What god of any nation has ever been able to save its people from my power? So what makes you think that the L*ORD can rescue Jerusalem from me?"* **2 KINGS 18:19, 35**

Reasons for hope that God will save my child:

My prayer for God to glorify himself through the salvation of my child:

Other prayer concerns today:

July 2

2 KINGS 20:1–22:2
ACTS 21:18-36
PSALM 150:1-6
PROVERBS 18:9-10

Isaiah said to Hezekiah, "Listen to this message from the LORD: The time is coming when everything in your palace—all the treasures stored up by your ancestors until now—will be carried off to Babylon. Nothing will be left, says the LORD. Some of your very own sons will be taken away into exile. They will become eunuchs who will serve in the palace of Babylon's king." Then Hezekiah said to Isaiah, "This message you have given me from the LORD is good." For the king was thinking, "At least there will be peace and security during my lifetime." **2 KINGS 20:16-19**

The impact I want to have in the lives of my children and grandchildren:

My prayer for the Lord to show me any selfishness in the way I parent:

Other prayer concerns today:

July 3

2 KINGS 22:3–23:30
ACTS 21:37–22:16
PSALM 1:1-6
PROVERBS 18:11-12

Oh, the joys of those who do not
follow the advice of the wicked,
or stand around with sinners,
or join in with mockers.
But they delight in the law of the LORD,
meditating on it day and night.
PSALM 1:1-2

Influences in my child's life I fear may lead him or her away from Christ:

My prayer for my child to reject the ideas, values, and behaviors of those who have rejected Christ:

Other prayer concerns today:

July 4

2 KINGS 23:31–25:30
ACTS 22:17–23:10
PSALM 2:1-12
PROVERBS 18:13

The king proclaims the LORD's decree:
"The LORD said to me, 'You are my son.
Today I have become your Father.
Only ask, and I will give you the nations as your inheritance,
the whole earth as your possession.'"
PSALM 2:7-8

The inheritance I hope to leave for my child:

My prayer of thanksgiving for being a part of the inheritance God has given to his Son:

Other prayer concerns today:

July 5

1 CHRONICLES 1:1–2:17
ACTS 23:11-35
PSALM 3:1-8
PROVERBS 18:14-15

The descendants of Adam were Seth, Enosh, Kenan, Mahalalel, Jared, Enoch, Methuselah, Lamech, and Noah. The sons of Noah were Shem, Ham, and Japheth. **1 CHRONICLES 1:1-4**

People included in the Old Testament's genealogy that give me hope:

My prayer for my child's identity to come from being a part of God's family by grace:

Other prayer concerns today:

July 6

1 CHRONICLES 2:18–4:4
ACTS 24:1-27
PSALM 4:1-8
PROVERBS 18:16-18

The descendants of Solomon were Rehoboam, Abijah, Asa, Jehoshaphat, Jehoram, Ahaziah, Joash, Amaziah, Uzziah, Jotham, Ahaz, Hezekiah, Manasseh, Amon, and Josiah. **1 CHRONICLES 3:10-14**

Confession of my desire for a formula or a guarantee that my child will take hold of Christ by faith:

My prayer for salvation from despair and from pride:

Other prayer concerns today:

July 7

1 CHRONICLES 4:5–5:17
ACTS 25:1-27
PSALM 5:1-12
PROVERBS 18:19

Let all who take refuge in you rejoice;
let them sing joyful praises forever.
Spread your protection over them,
that all who love your name may be filled with joy.
For you bless the godly, O Lord;
you surround them with your shield of love.
PSALM 5:11-12

Things I pray the Lord will protect my child from:

My prayer for the Lord to surround my child with his shield of love:

Other prayer concerns today:

July 8

1 CHRONICLES 5:18–6:81
ACTS 26:1-32
PSALM 6:1-10
PROVERBS 18:20-21

I am sick at heart.
How long, O Lord, until you restore me?
PSALM 6:3

Things I have been impatient for God to accomplish in our family:

My prayer of trust in God's timing as he works in our lives:

Other prayer concerns today:

July 9

1 CHRONICLES 7:1–8:40
ACTS 27:1-20
PSALM 7:1-17
PROVERBS 18:22

The man who finds a wife finds a treasure,
and he receives favor from the LORD.
PROVERBS 18:22

Qualities I pray my child will find in a spouse:

My prayer for my child to receive the favor of a godly spouse or the grace for singleness:

Other prayer concerns today:

July 10

1 CHRONICLES 9:1–10:14
ACTS 27:21-44
PSALM 8:1-9
PROVERBS 18:23-24

What are mere mortals that you should think about them,
human beings that you should care for them?
Yet you made them only a little lower than God
and crowned them with glory and honor.
You gave them charge of everything you made,
putting all things under their authority.
PSALM 8:4-6

What the world says about our value and purpose compared to what the Bible says:

My prayer for my child to embrace the destiny that really matters:

Other prayer concerns today:

July 11

1 CHRONICLES 11:1–12:18
ACTS 28:1-31
PSALM 9:1-12
PROVERBS 19:1-3

Better to be poor and honest
than to be dishonest and a fool.
PROVERBS 19:1

Ways I can model integrity to my child:

My prayer for my child to become a person of integrity:

Other prayer concerns today:

July 12

1 CHRONICLES 12:19–14:17
ROMANS 1:1-17
PSALM 9:13-20
PROVERBS 19:4-5

I am not ashamed of this Good News about Christ. It is the power of God at work, saving everyone who believes—the Jew first and also the Gentile. This Good News tells us how God makes us right in his sight. This is accomplished from start to finish by faith. As the Scriptures say, "It is through faith that a righteous person has life." **ROMANS 1:16-17**

Situations in which I find myself tempted to be ashamed of the gospel:

My prayer for greater confidence in the goodness of the gospel—and greater boldness to share it:

Other prayer concerns today:

July 13

1 CHRONICLES 15:1–16:36
ROMANS 1:18-32
PSALM 10:1-15
PROVERBS 19:6-7

The wrath of God is revealed from heaven against all ungodliness and unrighteousness of men, who by their unrighteousness suppress the truth. . . . And since they did not see fit to acknowledge God, God gave them up to a debased mind to do what ought not to be done. **ROMANS 1:18, 28, ESV**

My statement of determination not to give up:

My prayer for perseverance in praying for, standing with, and loving my child:

Other prayer concerns today:

July 14

1 CHRONICLES 16:37–18:17
ROMANS 2:1-24
PSALM 10:16-18
PROVERBS 19:8-9

God does not show favoritism. When the Gentiles sin, they will be destroyed, even though they never had God's written law. And the Jews, who do have God's law, will be judged by that law when they fail to obey it. . . . And this is the message I proclaim—that the day is coming when God, through Christ Jesus, will judge everyone's secret life. **ROMANS 2:11-12, 16**

Some of the ways I've been exposed to God's Word over my lifetime:

My prayer for my child to embrace the truth he or she has been given:

Other prayer concerns today:

July 15

1 CHRONICLES 19:1–21:30
ROMANS 2:25–3:8
PSALM 11:1-7
PROVERBS 19:10-12

Satan rose up against Israel and caused David to take a census of the people of Israel. So David said to Joab and the commanders of the army, "Take a census of all the people of Israel—from Beersheba in the south to Dan in the north—and bring me a report so I may know how many there are." **1 CHRONICLES 21:1-2**

Ways that pride might impact my parenting:

My prayer to put to death any pride that motivates my thoughts, actions, and attitudes:

Other prayer concerns today:

July 16

1 CHRONICLES 22:1–23:32
ROMANS 3:9-31
PSALM 12:1-8
PROVERBS 19:13-14

All have turned away; all have become useless. No one does good, not a single one. **ROMANS 3:12**

Ways I can communicate that the Christian life is not a system of rules but a welcome for sinners:

My prayer for the humility to become the chief repenter in our home:

Other prayer concerns today:

July 17

1 CHRONICLES 24:1–26:11
ROMANS 4:1-12
PSALM 13:1-6
PROVERBS 19:15-16

For the Scriptures tell us, "Abraham believed God, and God counted him as righteous because of his faith." When people work, their wages are not a gift, but something they have earned. But people are counted as righteous, not because of their work, but because of their faith in God who forgives sinners. **ROMANS 4:3-5**

Aspects of the real righteousness of Christ that have been deposited to my account as gifts:

My prayer for God to gift the righteousness of Christ to my child:

Other prayer concerns today:

July 18

1 CHRONICLES 26:12–27:34
ROMANS 4:13–5:5
PSALM 14:1-7
PROVERBS 19:17

We can rejoice, too, when we run into problems and trials, for we know that they help us develop endurance. And endurance develops strength of character, and character strengthens our confident hope of salvation. And this hope will not lead to disappointment. For we know how dearly God loves us, because he has given us the Holy Spirit to fill our hearts with his love. **ROMANS 5:3-5**

Aspects of parenting for which I need to develop endurance:

My prayer for God to use difficulties in our lives to develop endurance:

Other prayer concerns today:

July 19

1 CHRONICLES 28:1–29:30
ROMANS 5:6-21
PSALM 15:1-5
PROVERBS 19:18-19

Now, with God as our witness, and in the sight of all Israel—the LORD's assembly—I give you this charge. Be careful to obey all the commands of the LORD your God, so that you may continue to possess this good land and leave it to your children as a permanent inheritance. And Solomon, my son, learn to know the God of your ancestors intimately. Worship and serve him with your whole heart and a willing mind. **1 CHRONICLES 28:8-9**

Godly guidance I've given or need to give my child:

My prayer for my child to worship and serve the Lord with his or her whole heart and willing mind:

Other prayer concerns today:

July 20

2 CHRONICLES 1:1–3:17
ROMANS 6:1-23
PSALM 16:1-11
PROVERBS 19:20-21

Do not let any part of your body become an instrument of evil to serve sin. Instead, give yourselves completely to God, for you were dead, but now you have new life. So use your whole body as an instrument to do what is right for the glory of God. **ROMANS 6:13**

My prayer for my child to not let any part of his or her body become an instrument of evil to serve sin:

My prayer for my child to use his or her whole body as an instrument to do what is right for the glory of God:

Other prayer concerns today:

July 21

2 CHRONICLES 4:1–6:11
ROMANS 7:1-13
PSALM 17:1-15
PROVERBS 19:22-23

When we were controlled by our old nature, sinful desires were at work within us, and the law aroused these evil desires that produced a harvest of sinful deeds, resulting in death. But now we have been released from the law, for we died to it and are no longer captive to its power. Now we can serve God, not in the old way of obeying the letter of the law, but in the new way of living in the Spirit. **ROMANS 7:5-6**

My prayer for my child to experience the Spirit's power to change:

My prayer for my child to discover what it means to live in the Spirit:

Other prayer concerns today:

July 22

2 CHRONICLES 6:12–8:10
ROMANS 7:14–8:8
PSALM 18:1-15
PROVERBS 19:24-25

Now there is no condemnation for those who belong to Christ Jesus. **ROMANS 8:1**

Regrets over which I need to declare "no condemnation":

My prayer of gratitude that Christ has taken upon himself the condemnation I deserve:

Other prayer concerns today:

July 23

2 CHRONICLES 8:11–10:19
ROMANS 8:9-25
PSALM 18:16-36
PROVERBS 19:26

Against its will, all creation was subjected to God's curse. But with eager hope, the creation looks forward to the day when it will join God's children in glorious freedom from death and decay. For we know that all creation has been groaning as in the pains of childbirth right up to the present time. And we believers also groan, even though we have the Holy Spirit within us as a foretaste of future glory, for we long for our bodies to be released from sin and suffering. We, too, wait with eager hope for the day when God will give us our full rights as his adopted children, including the new bodies he has promised us. **ROMANS 8:20-23**

What it looks like to groan with eager hope in our circumstances:

My prayer of longing for Christ to come and end the curse's impact on this world:

Other prayer concerns today:

July 24

2 CHRONICLES 11:1–13:22
ROMANS 8:26-39
PSALM 18:37-50
PROVERBS 19:27-29

We know that God causes everything to work together for the good of those who love God and are called according to his purpose for them. For God knew his people in advance, and he chose them to become like his Son, so that his Son would be the firstborn among many brothers and sisters. **ROMANS 8:28-29**

Aspects of "everything" I sometimes struggle to believe God will use for good in my child's life:

My prayer of confidence that God *will* work everything together for my good and the good of my family:

Other prayer concerns today:

2 CHRONICLES 14:1–16:14
ROMANS 9:1-24
PSALM 19:1-14
PROVERBS 20:1

July 25

The instructions of the LORD are perfect, reviving the soul.
The decrees of the LORD are trustworthy, making wise the simple.
The commandments of the LORD are right, bringing joy to the heart.
The commands of the LORD are clear, giving insight for living.
Reverence for the LORD is pure, lasting forever.
The laws of the LORD are true; each one is fair.
They are more desirable than gold, even the finest gold.
They are sweeter than honey, even honey dripping from the comb.

PSALM 19:7-10

My prayer for my child to have a desire for God's Word:

My prayer that God's Word will impact my child as Psalm 19 promises:

Other prayer concerns today:

July 26

2 CHRONICLES 17:1–18:34
ROMANS 9:25–10:13
PSALM 20:1-9
PROVERBS 20:2-3

Some trust in chariots and some in horses,
but we trust in the name of the L*ORD* *our God.*
PSALM 20:7, ESV

Things in which I'm tempted to put my trust regarding my child's life, health, and growth:

My prayer of trust in the name of the Lord our God:

Other prayer concerns today:

July 27

2 CHRONICLES 19:1–20:37
ROMANS 10:14–11:12
PSALM 21:1-13
PROVERBS 20:4-6

Later Isaiah spoke boldly for God, saying, "I was found by people who were not looking for me. I showed myself to those who were not asking for me." But regarding Israel, God said, "All day long I opened my arms to them, but they were disobedient and rebellious." **ROMANS 10:20-21**

Blessings that await my child as he or she accepts Christ's embrace:

My prayer for my child to run into Christ's open arms:

Other prayer concerns today:

July 28

2 CHRONICLES 21:1–23:21
ROMANS 11:13-36
PSALM 22:1-18
PROVERBS 20:7

Oh, how great are God's riches and wisdom and knowledge! How impossible it is for us to understand his decisions and his ways! **ROMANS 11:33**

Things I don't fully understand but want to trust God with:

My prayer for my child to follow God's sometimes inscrutable ways:

Other prayer concerns today:

July 29

2 CHRONICLES 24:1–25:28
ROMANS 12:1-21
PSALM 22:19-31
PROVERBS 20:8-10

Don't copy the behavior and customs of this world, but let God transform you into a new person by changing the way you think. Then you will learn to know God's will for you, which is good and pleasing and perfect. **ROMANS 12:2**

My prayer for my child to be transformed by God rather than conformed to the world:

My prayer for my child to know God's will for his or her life:

Other prayer concerns today:

July 30

2 CHRONICLES 26:1–28:27
ROMANS 13:1-14
PSALM 23:1-6
PROVERBS 20:11

Everyone must submit to governing authorities. For all authority comes from God, and those in positions of authority have been placed there by God. So anyone who rebels against authority is rebelling against what God has instituted, and they will be punished. **ROMANS 13:1-2**

Ways I can model and train my child in appropriate submission to authority:

My prayer for the grace to submit to authority:

Other prayer concerns today:

July 31

2 CHRONICLES 29:1-36
ROMANS 14:1-23
PSALM 24:1-10
PROVERBS 20:12

Remember, we will all stand before the judgment seat of God. For the Scriptures say, "'As surely as I live,' says the LORD, 'every knee will bend to me, and every tongue will declare allegiance to God.'" Yes, each of us will give a personal account to God. **ROMANS 14:10-12**

Opportunities and resources I've had for which I will give an account to God:

My prayer seeking forgiveness for the way I've judged others:

Other prayer concerns today:

August 1

2 CHRONICLES 30:1–31:21
ROMANS 15:1-22
PSALM 25:1-15
PROVERBS 20:13-15

Therefore, accept each other just as Christ has accepted you so that God will be given glory. **ROMANS 15:7**

Things I struggle to accept in others:

My prayer for grace to accept others in the way Christ has accepted me:

Other prayer concerns today:

August 2

2 CHRONICLES 32:1–33:13
ROMANS 15:23–16:9
PSALM 25:16-22
PROVERBS 20:16-18

While in deep distress, Manasseh sought the LORD his God and sincerely humbled himself before the God of his ancestors. And when he prayed, the LORD listened to him and was moved by his request. So the LORD brought Manasseh back to Jerusalem and to his kingdom. Then Manasseh finally realized that the LORD alone is God! **2 CHRONICLES 33:12-13**

Things about God I don't want my child to forget:

My prayer for my child to be confident in the mercy of God:

Other prayer concerns today:

August 3

2 CHRONICLES 33:14–34:33
ROMANS 16:10-27
PSALM 26:1-12
PROVERBS 20:19

Declare me innocent, O LORD,
for I have acted with integrity;
I have trusted in the LORD without wavering.
Put me on trial, LORD, and cross-examine me.
Test my motives and my heart.
For I am always aware of your unfailing love,
and I have lived according to your truth.
PSALM 26:1-3

Ways I'd like to see God close the gap between his character and my own:

My prayer of gratitude for grace that enables me to welcome God's examination:

Other prayer concerns today:

August 4

2 CHRONICLES 35:1–36:23
1 CORINTHIANS 1:1-17
PSALM 27:1-6
PROVERBS 20:20-21

All the leaders of the priests and the people became more and more unfaithful. They followed all the pagan practices of the surrounding nations, desecrating the Temple of the LORD that had been consecrated in Jerusalem. The LORD, the God of their ancestors, repeatedly sent his prophets to warn them, for he had compassion on his people and his Temple. But the people mocked these messengers of God and despised their words. They scoffed at the prophets until the LORD's anger could no longer be restrained and nothing could be done. **2 CHRONICLES 36:14-16**

Ways I can show God-like faithfulness and compassion to my child:

My prayer of praise to God for relentlessly pursuing relationship with his people:

Other prayer concerns today:

August 5

EZRA 1:1–2:70
1 CORINTHIANS 1:18–2:5
PSALM 27:7-14
PROVERBS 20:22-23

God stirred the hearts of the priests and Levites and the leaders of the tribes of Judah and Benjamin to go to Jerusalem to rebuild the Temple of the L*ORD.* **EZRA 1:5**

Ways I'd like to see God stir the heart of my child:

My prayer asking God to stir the heart of my child to long for him:

Other prayer concerns today:

August 6

EZRA 3:1–4:23
1 CORINTHIANS 2:6–3:4
PSALM 28:1-9
PROVERBS 20:24-25

It was to us that God revealed these things by his Spirit. For his Spirit searches out everything and shows us God's deep secrets. No one can know a person's thoughts except that person's own spirit, and no one can know God's thoughts except God's own Spirit. And we have received God's Spirit (not the world's spirit), so we can know the wonderful things God has freely given us. **1 CORINTHIANS 2:10-12**

Wisdom from the world that inundates my child's life:

My prayer for the wisdom of God's Spirit to shape my child's thoughts and attitudes:

Other prayer concerns today:

August 7

EZRA 4:24–6:22
1 CORINTHIANS 3:5-23
PSALM 29:1-11
PROVERBS 20:26-27

The voice of the LORD echoes above the sea.
The God of glory thunders.
The LORD thunders over the mighty sea.
The voice of the LORD is powerful;
the voice of the LORD is majestic.
The voice of the LORD splits the mighty cedars;
the LORD shatters the cedars of Lebanon.
PSALM 29:3-5

Voices in my child's life that I would like to have less power so that he or she can hear the voice of the Lord:

My prayer for the voice of the Lord to be heard in our family:

Other prayer concerns today:

August 8

EZRA 7:1–8:20
1 CORINTHIANS 4:1-21
PSALM 30:1-12
PROVERBS 20:28-30

As for me, it matters very little how I might be evaluated by you or by any human authority. I don't even trust my own judgment on this point. My conscience is clear, but that doesn't prove I'm right. It is the Lord himself who will examine me and decide. **1 CORINTHIANS 4:3-4**

Voices of evaluation in my child's life:

My prayer for my child to be saved from the weight of the evaluation of self and others:

Other prayer concerns today:

August 9

EZRA 8:21–9:15
1 CORINTHIANS 5:1-13
PSALM 31:1-8
PROVERBS 21:1-2

It isn't my responsibility to judge outsiders, but it certainly is your responsibility to judge those inside the church who are sinning. **1 CORINTHIANS 5:12**

Attitudes or behaviors in my child that may call for compassionate confrontation:

My prayer for increasing love for the purity of Christ's church:

Other prayer concerns today:

August 10

EZRA 10:1-44
1 CORINTHIANS 6:1-20
PSALM 31:9-18
PROVERBS 21:3

Run from sexual sin! No other sin so clearly affects the body as this one does. For sexual immorality is a sin against your own body. Don't you realize that your body is the temple of the Holy Spirit, who lives in you and was given to you by God? You do not belong to yourself, for God bought you with a high price. So you must honor God with your body. **1 CORINTHIANS 6:18-20**

My prayer for God to instill in me and my child a desire to honor God with our bodies:

My prayer for the ability to helpfully articulate the holiness and significance of sex to my child:

Other prayer concerns today:

August 11

NEHEMIAH 1:1–3:14
1 CORINTHIANS 7:1-24
PSALM 31:19-24
PROVERBS 21:4

I asked them about the Jews who had returned there from captivity and about how things were going in Jerusalem. They said to me, "Things are not going well for those who returned to the province of Judah. They are in great trouble and disgrace. The wall of Jerusalem has been torn down, and the gates have been destroyed by fire." When I heard this, I sat down and wept. In fact, for days I mourned, fasted, and prayed to the God of heaven. **NEHEMIAH 1:2-4**

Prayers I can pray when my child is in "great trouble and disgrace":

My prayer for the things that break God's heart to break my heart:

Other prayer concerns today:

August 12

NEHEMIAH 3:15–5:13
1 CORINTHIANS 7:25-40
PSALM 32:1-11
PROVERBS 21:5-7

About this time some of the men and their wives raised a cry of protest against their fellow Jews. They were saying, "We have such large families. We need more food to survive." Others said, "We have mortgaged our fields, vineyards, and homes to get food during the famine." . . . When I heard their complaints, I was very angry. **NEHEMIAH 5:1-3, 6**

Things I've become angry over in recent days:

My prayer for the grace to model appropriate anger in our home:

Other prayer concerns today:

August 13

NEHEMIAH 5:14–7:73a
1 CORINTHIANS 8:1-13
PSALM 33:1-11
PROVERBS 21:8-10

It is better to live in a corner of the housetop
than in a house shared with a quarrelsome wife.
PROVERBS 21:9, ESV

The kinds of words that set the tenor of our home for good or ill:

My prayer for our family to speak to one another with kindness:

Other prayer concerns today:

August 14

NEHEMIAH 7:73b–9:21
1 CORINTHIANS 9:1-18
PSALM 33:12-22
PROVERBS 21:11-12

In October, when the Israelites had settled in their towns, all the people assembled with a unified purpose at the square just inside the Water Gate. They asked Ezra the scribe to bring out the Book of the Law of Moses, which the LORD had given for Israel to obey. So on October 8 Ezra the priest brought the Book of the Law before the assembly, which included the men and women and all the children old enough to understand. He faced the square just inside the Water Gate from early morning until noon and read aloud to everyone who could understand. All the people listened closely to the Book of the Law. **NEHEMIAH 7:73–8:3**

Hindrances that keep our family from gathering with God's people and listening closely to his Word:

My prayer for greater understanding of God's Word in our family:

Other prayer concerns today:

August 15

NEHEMIAH 9:22–10:39
1 CORINTHIANS 9:19–10:13
PSALM 34:1-10
PROVERBS 21:13

If you think you are standing strong, be careful not to fall. The temptations in your life are no different from what others experience. And God is faithful. He will not allow the temptation to be more than you can stand. When you are tempted, he will show you a way out so that you can endure. **1 CORINTHIANS 10:12-13**

Good things that threaten to become ultimate things in our lives:

My prayer for the Spirit to reveal anything I have come to love and depend on more than God:

Other prayer concerns today:

August 16

NEHEMIAH 11:1–12:26
1 CORINTHIANS 10:14-33
PSALM 34:11-22
PROVERBS 21:14-16

Come, my children, and listen to me,
and I will teach you to fear the LORD*.*
PSALM 34:11

Evidence I often care more about what other people think of me than what God thinks of me:

My prayer for the ability to encourage the fear of the Lord in my child's life:

Other prayer concerns today:

August 17

NEHEMIAH 12:27–13:31
1 CORINTHIANS 11:1-16
PSALM 35:1-16
PROVERBS 21:17-18

I was not in Jerusalem at that time, for I had returned to King Artaxerxes of Babylon in the thirty-second year of his reign, though I later asked his permission to return. When I arrived back in Jerusalem, I learned about Eliashib's evil deed in providing Tobiah with a room in the courtyards of the Temple of God. I became very upset and threw all of Tobiah's belongings out of the room. **NEHEMIAH 13:6-8**

Ways I try to guard our family from compromise with the world:

My prayer for the protection only God can provide against compromise:

Other prayer concerns today:

August 18

ESTHER 1:1–3:15
1 CORINTHIANS 11:17-34
PSALM 35:17-28
PROVERBS 21:19-20

Anyone who eats this bread or drinks this cup of the Lord unworthily is guilty of sinning against the body and blood of the Lord. That is why you should examine yourself before eating the bread and drinking the cup. For if you eat the bread or drink the cup without honoring the body of Christ, you are eating and drinking God's judgment upon yourself. **1 CORINTHIANS 11:27-29**

My understanding of what it means to take the Lord's Supper in an unworthy manner:

My prayer for the ability to communicate what is true and right about the Lord's Supper to my child:

Other prayer concerns today:

August 19

ESTHER 4:1–7:10
1 CORINTHIANS 12:1-26
PSALM 36:1-12
PROVERBS 21:21-22

Mordecai sent this reply to Esther: "Don't think for a moment that because you're in the palace you will escape when all other Jews are killed. If you keep quiet at a time like this, deliverance and relief for the Jews will arise from some other place, but you and your relatives will die. Who knows if perhaps you were made queen for just such a time as this?" **ESTHER 4:13-14**

Situations in which I want to boldly identify myself as part of God's people:

My prayer for my child to have the courage to stand out as belonging to Christ:

Other prayer concerns today:

August 20

ESTHER 8:1–10:3
1 CORINTHIANS 12:27–13:13
PSALM 37:1-11
PROVERBS 21:23-24

Love never gives up, never loses faith, is always hopeful.
1 CORINTHIANS 13:7

Aspects of this verse from 1 Corinthians that are particularly important for me:

My prayer to love my child in a way that reflects a 1 Corinthians 13 kind of love:

Other prayer concerns today:

August 21

JOB 1:1–3:26
1 CORINTHIANS 14:1-17
PSALM 37:12-29
PROVERBS 21:25-26

Job's sons would take turns preparing feasts in their homes, and they would also invite their three sisters to celebrate with them. When these celebrations ended—sometimes after several days—Job would purify his children. He would get up early in the morning and offer a burnt offering for each of them. For Job said to himself, "Perhaps my children have sinned and have cursed God in their hearts." This was Job's regular practice. **JOB 1:4-5**

My fears about what might be happening in the heart of my child:

My prayer for God to do a purifying work in my child's heart:

Other prayer concerns today:

JOB 4:1–7:21

1 CORINTHIANS 14:18-40

PSALM 37:30-40

PROVERBS 21:27

August 22

The godly offer good counsel;
they teach right from wrong.
They have made God's law their own,
so they will never slip from his path.

PSALM 37:30-31

The way I want my children to describe my parenting:

My prayer to be a godly parent:

Other prayer concerns today:

August 23

JOB 8:1–11:20
1 CORINTHIANS 15:1-28
PSALM 38:1-22
PROVERBS 21:28-29

You claim, "My beliefs are pure,"
and "I am clean in the sight of God." . . .
Listen! God is doubtless punishing you
far less than you deserve!
JOB 11:4, 6

The reason I can be sure that my suffering is not God punishing me for my sin:

My prayer for me and my child to grasp the goodness of the gospel:

Other prayer concerns today:

August 24

JOB 12:1–15:35
1 CORINTHIANS 15:29-58
PSALM 39:1-13
PROVERBS 21:30-31

My dear brothers and sisters, be strong and immovable. Always work enthusiastically for the Lord, for you know that nothing you do for the Lord is ever useless. **1 CORINTHIANS 15:58**

Grounds for confidence that my parenting to the glory of God matters beyond this life:

My prayer to be strong and immovable in my parenting work for the Lord:

Other prayer concerns today:

August 25

JOB 16:1–19:29
1 CORINTHIANS 16:1-24
PSALM 40:1-10
PROVERBS 22:1

What miserable comforters you are!
Won't you ever stop blowing hot air?
What makes you keep on talking?
I could say the same things if you were in my place.
I could spout off criticism and shake my head at you.
But if it were me, I would encourage you.
I would try to take away your grief.

JOB 16:2-5

Words I could use to come alongside my child when he or she is hurting:

My prayer for growth in being a genuine encourager to my child in hard places of life:

Other prayer concerns today:

JOB 20:1–22:30
2 CORINTHIANS 1:1-11
PSALM 40:11-17
PROVERBS 22:2-4

August 26

We think you ought to know, dear brothers and sisters, about the trouble we went through in the province of Asia. We were crushed and overwhelmed beyond our ability to endure, and we thought we would never live through it. In fact, we expected to die. But as a result, we stopped relying on ourselves and learned to rely only on God, who raises the dead. **2 CORINTHIANS 1:8-9**

My anxieties about becoming more God-reliant and less self-reliant:

My prayer to learn to depend on God, who raises the dead:

Other prayer concerns today:

August 27

JOB 23:1–27:23
2 CORINTHIANS 1:12–2:11
PSALM 41:1-13
PROVERBS 22:5-6

Direct your children onto the right path,
and when they are older, they will not leave it.
PROVERBS 22:6

What I can do to direct my child onto the right path:

My prayer of petition that the Lord will bring about the repentance and faith in my child's life as only he can:

Other prayer concerns today:

JOB 28:1–30:31

2 CORINTHIANS 2:12-17

PSALM 42:1-11

PROVERBS 22:7

August 28

Why am I discouraged?
Why is my heart so sad?
I will put my hope in God!
I will praise him again—
my Savior and my God!

PSALM 42:5-6

My encouragement to my own soul to hope in God:

My prayer for God to save me from discouragement and despair in parenting:

Other prayer concerns today:

August 29

JOB 31:1–33:33
2 CORINTHIANS 3:1-18
PSALM 43:1-5
PROVERBS 22:8-9

I made a covenant with my eyes
not to look with lust at a young woman.
For what has God above chosen for us?
What is our inheritance from the Almighty on high?
Isn't it calamity for the wicked
and misfortune for those who do evil?
Doesn't he see everything I do
and every step I take?
JOB 31:1-4

Strategies for fighting the battle for purity in our home:

My prayer for me and my child to stay in the fight against lust:

Other prayer concerns today:

August 30

JOB 34:1–36:33
2 CORINTHIANS 4:1-12
PSALM 44:1-8
PROVERBS 22:10-12

Satan, who is the god of this world, has blinded the minds of those who don't believe. They are unable to see the glorious light of the Good News. They don't understand this message about the glory of Christ, who is the exact likeness of God. . . . For God, who said, "Let there be light in the darkness," has made this light shine in our hearts so we could know the glory of God that is seen in the face of Jesus Christ. **2 CORINTHIANS 4:4, 6**

Lies of Satan I don't want my child to believe:

My prayer for my child to see the glory of God in the face of Jesus Christ:

Other prayer concerns today:

August 31

JOB 37:1–39:30
2 CORINTHIANS 4:13–5:10
PSALM 44:9-26
PROVERBS 22:13

That is why we never give up. Though our bodies are dying, our spirits are being renewed every day. For our present troubles are small and won't last very long. Yet they produce for us a glory that vastly outweighs them and will last forever! So we don't look at the troubles we can see now; rather, we fix our gaze on things that cannot be seen. For the things we see now will soon be gone, but the things we cannot see will last forever. **2 CORINTHIANS 4:16-18**

Reasons and ways I'm sometimes tempted to give up:

My prayer to fix my gaze on spiritual realities that I can't see with my physical eyes:

Other prayer concerns today:

September 1

JOB 40:1–42:17
2 CORINTHIANS 5:11-21
PSALM 45:1-17
PROVERBS 22:14

God . . . brought us back to himself through Christ. And God has given us this task of reconciling people to him. For God was in Christ, reconciling the world to himself, no longer counting people's sins against them. And he gave us this wonderful message of reconciliation. So we are Christ's ambassadors; God is making his appeal through us. We speak for Christ when we plead, "Come back to God!" **2 CORINTHIANS 5:18-20**

What it would mean for me to have a message of reconciliation rather than condemnation for my child:

My prayer to live in our home as a reconciler:

Other prayer concerns today:

September 2

ECCLESIASTES 1:1–3:22
2 CORINTHIANS 6:1-13
PSALM 46:1-11
PROVERBS 22:15

"Everything is meaningless," says the Teacher, "completely meaningless!"
ECCLESIASTES 1:2

Ways I pray my life will matter beyond my limited lifetime:

My prayer for Christ to fill my child's life with meaning and purpose:

Other prayer concerns today:

ECCLESIASTES 4:1–6:12
2 CORINTHIANS 6:14–7:7
PSALM 47:1-9
PROVERBS 22:16

September 3

Because we have these promises, dear friends, let us cleanse ourselves from everything that can defile our body or spirit. And let us work toward complete holiness because we fear God. **2 CORINTHIANS 7:1**

Things parenting has shown me about myself:

My prayer for my life and my child's life to be marked by increasing holiness:

Other prayer concerns today:

September 4

ECCLESIASTES 7:1–9:18
2 CORINTHIANS 7:8-16
PSALM 48:1-14
PROVERBS 22:17-19

I am not sorry that I sent that severe letter to you, though I was sorry at first, for I know it was painful to you for a little while. Now I am glad I sent it, not because it hurt you, but because the pain caused you to repent and change your ways. It was the kind of sorrow God wants his people to have, so you were not harmed by us in any way. For the kind of sorrow God wants us to experience leads us away from sin and results in salvation. There's no regret for that kind of sorrow. But worldly sorrow, which lacks repentance, results in spiritual death. **2 CORINTHIANS 7:8-10**

Sins over which I want to experience godly sorrow:

My prayer for my child to experience the spiritual health that is a result of godly sorrow:

Other prayer concerns today:

ECCLESIASTES 10:1–12:14
2 CORINTHIANS 8:1-15
PSALM 49:1-20
PROVERBS 22:20-21

September 5

Here now is my final conclusion: Fear God and obey his commands, for this is everyone's duty. God will judge us for everything we do, including every secret thing, whether good or bad. **ECCLESIASTES 12:13-14**

Clear commands from God I want to be sure to obey today:

My prayer of gratitude that Christ has saved me from being judged for every secret bad thing I have done:

Other prayer concerns today:

September 6

SONG OF SONGS 1:1–4:16
2 CORINTHIANS 8:16-24
PSALM 50:1-23
PROVERBS 22:22-23

Promise me, O women of Jerusalem,
by the gazelles and wild deer,
not to awaken love until the time is right.
SONG OF SONGS 2:7

Ways I'd like to communicate the good gift God intends sexual love to be as well as the boundaries he has set for it:

My prayer for my child to experience sexual love as a good gift protected by marriage:

Other prayer concerns today:

SONG OF SONGS 5:1–8:14
2 CORINTHIANS 9:1-15
PSALM 51:1-19
PROVERBS 22:24-25

September 7

Place me like a seal over your heart,
like a seal on your arm.
For love is as strong as death,
its jealousy as enduring as the grave.
Love flashes like fire,
the brightest kind of flame.
Many waters cannot quench love,
nor can rivers drown it.
If a man tried to buy love
with all his wealth,
his offer would be utterly scorned.

SONG OF SONGS 8:6-7

Ways in which I desire my child to experience love sealed through lifelong commitment:

My prayer for my child to experience the healing of sexual wounds and scars, something only Christ can provide:

Other prayer concerns today:

September 8

ISAIAH 1:1–2:22
2 CORINTHIANS 10:1-18
PSALM 52:1-9
PROVERBS 22:26-27

We are human, but we don't wage war as humans do. We use God's mighty weapons, not worldly weapons, to knock down the strongholds of human reasoning and to destroy false arguments. We destroy every proud obstacle that keeps people from knowing God. We capture their rebellious thoughts and teach them to obey Christ. **2 CORINTHIANS 10:3-5**

Human reasoning, false arguments, proud obstacles, or rebellious thoughts that threaten our home:

My prayer to use God's mighty weapons rather than worldly weapons in the battle for the spiritual health of our family:

Other prayer concerns today:

ISAIAH 3:1–5:30
2 CORINTHIANS 11:1-15
PSALM 53:1-6
PROVERBS 22:28-29

September 9

My beloved had a vineyard
on a rich and fertile hill.
He plowed the land, cleared its stones,
and planted it with the best vines.
In the middle he built a watchtower
and carved a winepress in the nearby rocks.
Then he waited for a harvest of sweet grapes,
but the grapes that grew were bitter.

ISAIAH 5:1-2

How it helps me to know that God has raised children who rebelled:

My prayer for my child to be grafted in and abide in the true vine of Christ:

Other prayer concerns today:

September 10

ISAIAH 6:1–7:25
2 CORINTHIANS 11:16-33
PSALM 54:1-7
PROVERBS 23:1-3

Then I said, "It's all over! I am doomed, for I am a sinful man. I have filthy lips, and I live among a people with filthy lips. Yet I have seen the King, the LORD of Heaven's Armies." Then one of the seraphim flew to me with a burning coal he had taken from the altar with a pair of tongs. He touched my lips with it and said, "See, this coal has touched your lips. Now your guilt is removed, and your sins are forgiven." **ISAIAH 6:5-7**

The strengths in my child that I want to recognize and affirm even as his or her ultimate identity is found in Christ:

My prayer for wisdom to know how to encourage and affirm my child's strengths:

Other prayer concerns today:

September 11

ISAIAH 8:1–9:21
2 CORINTHIANS 12:1-10
PSALM 55:1-23
PROVERBS 23:4-5

To keep me from becoming proud, I was given a thorn in my flesh, a messenger from Satan to torment me and keep me from becoming proud. Three different times I begged the Lord to take it away. Each time he said, "My grace is all you need. My power works best in weakness." So now I am glad to boast about my weaknesses, so that the power of Christ can work through me. That's why I take pleasure in my weaknesses, and in the insults, hardships, persecutions, and troubles that I suffer for Christ. For when I am weak, then I am strong. **2 CORINTHIANS 12:7-10**

Pain I would like God to remove:

My prayer for sufficient grace to endure the pain he does not take away:

Other prayer concerns today:

September 12

ISAIAH 10:1–11:16
2 CORINTHIANS 12:11-21
PSALM 56:1-13
PROVERBS 23:6-8

I am coming to you for the third time, and I will not be a burden to you. I don't want what you have—I want you. After all, children don't provide for their parents. Rather, parents provide for their children. I will gladly spend myself and all I have for you, even though it seems that the more I love you, the less you love me. **2 CORINTHIANS 12:14-15**

Ways I have "spent myself" for my child:

My prayer for the Spirit of Christ, who spent himself for me, to empower me to spend myself for others:

Other prayer concerns today:

September 13

ISAIAH 12:1–14:32
2 CORINTHIANS 13:1-14
PSALM 57:1-11
PROVERBS 23:9-11

Examine yourselves to see if your faith is genuine. Test yourselves. Surely you know that Jesus Christ is among you; if not, you have failed the test of genuine faith. **2 CORINTHIANS 13:5**

Signs of genuine faith I want to be evident in my life and my child's life:

My prayer for my child to pass the test for authentic faith:

Other prayer concerns today:

September 14

ISAIAH 15:1–18:7
GALATIANS 1:1-24
PSALM 58:1-11
PROVERBS 23:12

Let God's curse fall on anyone, including us or even an angel from heaven, who preaches a different kind of Good News than the one we preached to you. I say again what we have said before: If anyone preaches any other Good News than the one you welcomed, let that person be cursed. Obviously, I'm not trying to win the approval of people, but of God. If pleasing people were my goal, I would not be Christ's servant. **GALATIANS 1:8-10**

Sources from which my child seeks approval:

My prayer for my child to experience the approval of God that comes from being joined to Christ:

Other prayer concerns today:

ISAIAH 19:1–21:17
GALATIANS 2:1-16
PSALM 59:1-17
PROVERBS 23:13-14

September 15

Don't fail to discipline your children.
The rod of punishment won't kill them.
Physical discipline
may well save them from death.
PROVERBS 23:13-14

Marks of disciplining my child in a godly and grace-filled way:

My prayer to discipline my child in a reasoned and purposeful way:

Other prayer concerns today:

September 16

ISAIAH 22:1–24:23
GALATIANS 2:17–3:9
PSALM 60:1-12
PROVERBS 23:15-16

My old self has been crucified with Christ. It is no longer I who live, but Christ lives in me. So I live in this earthly body by trusting in the Son of God, who loved me and gave himself for me. I do not treat the grace of God as meaningless. For if keeping the law could make us right with God, then there was no need for Christ to die. **GALATIANS 2:20-21**

How I want my child to see himself or herself:

My prayer for my child to increasingly define himself or herself by connectedness to Christ:

Other prayer concerns today:

September 17

ISAIAH 25:1–28:13
GALATIANS 3:10-22
PSALM 61:1-8
PROVERBS 23:17-18

Those who depend on the law to make them right with God are under his curse, for the Scriptures say, "Cursed is everyone who does not observe and obey all the commands that are written in God's Book of the Law." So it is clear that no one can be made right with God by trying to keep the law. For the Scriptures say, "It is through faith that a righteous person has life." This way of faith is very different from the way of law, which says, "It is through obeying the law that a person has life." **GALATIANS 3:10-12**

My understanding of the difference between the way of faith and the way of law:

My prayer for my child to want to live a holy life and for dependance on Christ's power to do so:

Other prayer concerns today:

September 18

ISAIAH 28:14–30:11
GALATIANS 3:23–4:31
PSALM 62:1-12
PROVERBS 23:19-21

When the right time came, God sent his Son, born of a woman, subject to the law. God sent him to buy freedom for us who were slaves to the law, so that he could adopt us as his very own children. And because we are his children, God has sent the Spirit of his Son into our hearts, prompting us to call out, "Abba, Father." Now you are no longer a slave but God's own child. And since you are his child, God has made you his heir. **GALATIANS 4:4-7**

Ways that God is a better parent to my child than I will ever be:

My prayer for my child to inherit everything God intends to give to him or her:

Other prayer concerns today:

ISAIAH 30:12–33:9
GALATIANS 5:1-12
PSALM 63:1-11
PROVERBS 23:22

September 19

O God, you are my God;
I earnestly search for you.
My soul thirsts for you;
my whole body longs for you
in this parched and weary land
where there is no water.
PSALM 63:1

Ways I can stir up longing for God in my own soul:

My prayer to experience the nearness of God in desperate circumstances:

Other prayer concerns today:

September 20

ISAIAH 33:10–36:22
GALATIANS 5:13-25
PSALM 64:1-10
PROVERBS 23:23

The Holy Spirit produces this kind of fruit in our lives: love, joy, peace, patience, kindness, goodness, faithfulness, gentleness, and self-control. **GALATIANS 5:22-23**

Spiritual fruit I long to see in my child's life:

My prayer for the fruit of the Spirit to mark my relationship to my child:

Other prayer concerns today:

September 21

ISAIAH 37:1–38:22
GALATIANS 6:1-18
PSALM 65:1-13
PROVERBS 23:24

Don't be misled—you cannot mock the justice of God. You will always harvest what you plant. Those who live only to satisfy their own sinful nature will harvest decay and death from that sinful nature. But those who live to please the Spirit will harvest everlasting life from the Spirit. So let's not get tired of doing what is good. At just the right time we will reap a harvest of blessing if we don't give up. **GALATIANS 6:7-9**

What I think it looks like to live to please the Spirit:

My prayer for endurance to keep on doing what is good:

Other prayer concerns today:

September 22

ISAIAH 39:1–41:16
EPHESIANS 1:1-23
PSALM 66:1-20
PROVERBS 23:25-28

Christ . . . fills all things everywhere with himself.
EPHESIANS 1:23

Spiritual blessings from Ephesians 1 that I pray will be given to my child:

My prayer for my child to be given spiritual wisdom and insight to grow in the knowledge of God:

Other prayer concerns today:

September 23

ISAIAH 41:17–43:13
EPHESIANS 2:1-22
PSALM 67:1-7
PROVERBS 23:29-35

Once you were dead because of your disobedience and your many sins. You used to live in sin, just like the rest of the world, obeying the devil—the commander of the powers in the unseen world. He is the spirit at work in the hearts of those who refuse to obey God. All of us used to live that way, following the passionate desires and inclinations of our sinful nature. By our very nature we were subject to God's anger, just like everyone else. But God is so rich in mercy, and he loved us so much, that even though we were dead because of our sins, he gave us life when he raised Christ from the dead. (It is only by God's grace that you have been saved!) For he raised us from the dead along with Christ and seated us with him in the heavenly realms because we are united with Christ Jesus. So God can point to us in all future ages as examples of the incredible wealth of his grace and kindness toward us, as shown in all he has done for us who are united with Christ Jesus. **EPHESIANS 2:1-7**

My confession of my inability to generate spiritual life in my child:

My prayer for my child to be made alive by becoming joined to Christ:

Other prayer concerns today:

September 24

ISAIAH 43:14–45:10
EPHESIANS 3:1-21
PSALM 68:1-18
PROVERBS 24:1-2

I pray that from his glorious, unlimited resources he will empower you with inner strength through his Spirit. Then Christ will make his home in your hearts as you trust in him. Your roots will grow down into God's love and keep you strong. **EPHESIANS 3:16-17**

Areas in my child's life in which I'd like to see Christ making his home:

My prayer for my child to grow deep roots in the love of God that will keep him or her strong:

Other prayer concerns today:

September 25

ISAIAH 45:11–48:11
EPHESIANS 4:1-16
PSALM 68:19-35
PROVERBS 24:3-4

Let all the world look to me for salvation!
For I am God; there is no other. . . .
The people will declare,
"The LORD is the source of all my righteousness and strength."
ISAIAH 45:22, 24

What it looks like to live as a person who recognizes the Lord as the source of all my righteousness and strength:

My prayer for my child to look to Christ for salvation, righteousness, and strength:

Other prayer concerns today:

September 26

ISAIAH 48:12–50:11
EPHESIANS 4:17-32
PSALM 69:1-18
PROVERBS 24:5-6

Let the Spirit renew your thoughts and attitudes.
EPHESIANS 4:23

Aspects of the new nature I long to see in my child:

My prayer that the old nature would be increasingly thrown off and the new nature would be increasingly put on in my child's life:

Other prayer concerns today:

September 27

ISAIAH 51:1–53:12
EPHESIANS 5:1-33
PSALM 69:19-36
PROVERBS 24:7

Be imitators of God, as beloved children . . . for at one time you were darkness, but now you are light in the Lord. Walk as children of light. **EPHESIANS 5:1, 8, ESV**

Areas in which I'd like my child to find his or her identity in being a son or daughter of God:

My prayer for my child to be miserable when participating in what belongs to darkness:

Other prayer concerns today:

September 28

ISAIAH 54:1–57:14
EPHESIANS 6:1-24
PSALM 70:1-5
PROVERBS 24:8

Fathers, do not provoke your children to anger by the way you treat them. Rather, bring them up with the discipline and instruction that comes from the Lord. **EPHESIANS 6:4**

The kind of discipline and instruction that comes from the Lord:

My prayer to discipline and instruct my child in this way:

Other prayer concerns today:

September 29

ISAIAH 57:15–59:21
PHILIPPIANS 1:1-26
PSALM 71:1-24
PROVERBS 24:9-10

Every time I think of you, I give thanks to my God. Whenever I pray, I make my requests for all of you with joy, for you have been my partners in spreading the Good News about Christ from the time you first heard it until now. And I am certain that God, who began the good work within you, will continue his work until it is finally finished on the day when Christ Jesus returns. **PHILIPPIANS 1:3-6**

Ways I'd like to see God continue his work in my child until it is finished:

My prayer for patience and faith that God is at work, even when I can't see it:

Other prayer concerns today:

September 30

ISAIAH 60:1–62:5
PHILIPPIANS 1:27–2:18
PSALM 72:1-20
PROVERBS 24:11-12

Don't be selfish; don't try to impress others. Be humble, thinking of others as better than yourselves. Don't look out only for your own interests, but take an interest in others, too. You must have the same attitude that Christ Jesus had.

Though he was God,
he did not think of equality with God
as something to cling to.
Instead, he gave up his divine privileges;
he took the humble position of a slave
and was born as a human being.
When he appeared in human form,
he humbled himself in obedience to God
and died a criminal's death on a cross.

PHILIPPIANS 2:3-8

Christlike attitudes I long to see in myself and my child:

My prayer for myself and my child to have our attitudes conformed to Christ:

Other prayer concerns today:

October 1

ISAIAH 62:6–65:25
PHILIPPIANS 2:19–3:3
PSALM 73:1-28
PROVERBS 24:13-14

Truly God is good to Israel,
to those whose hearts are pure.
But as for me, I almost lost my footing.
My feet were slipping, and I was almost gone.
For I envied the proud
when I saw them prosper despite their wickedness.
PSALM 73:1-3

How we're doing at making corporate worship a priority in our family:

My prayer for weekly worship to shape how we think about what is true, real, and eternal:

Other prayer concerns today:

October 2

ISAIAH 66:1-24
PHILIPPIANS 3:4-21
PSALM 74:1-23
PROVERBS 24:15-16

I focus on this one thing: Forgetting the past and looking forward to what lies ahead, I press on to reach the end of the race and receive the heavenly prize for which God, through Christ Jesus, is calling us. **PHILIPPIANS 3:13-14**

Issues or pursuits in our family that need to be seen through an eternal perspective:

My prayer to reach the new creation together as a family:

Other prayer concerns today:

October 3

JEREMIAH 1:1–2:30
PHILIPPIANS 4:1-23
PSALM 75:1-10
PROVERBS 24:17-20

Don't worry about anything; instead, pray about everything. Tell God what you need, and thank him for all he has done. Then you will experience God's peace, which exceeds anything we can understand. His peace will guard your hearts and minds as you live in Christ Jesus. **PHILIPPIANS 4:6-7**

Things I worry about that I want to pray about instead:

My prayer for anxiety to give way to hope in my heart and mind:

Other prayer concerns today:

October 4

JEREMIAH 2:31–4:18
COLOSSIANS 1:1-17
PSALM 76:1-12
PROVERBS 24:21-22

We have not stopped praying for you since we first heard about you. We ask God to give you complete knowledge of his will and to give you spiritual wisdom and understanding. Then the way you live will always honor and please the Lord, and your lives will produce every kind of good fruit. All the while, you will grow as you learn to know God better and better. **COLOSSIANS 1:9-10**

Specific areas where I'd like to see God give my child knowledge of his will, spiritual wisdom, and understanding:

My prayer for every kind of good fruit to be produced in my child's life:

Other prayer concerns today:

October 5

JEREMIAH 4:19–6:15
COLOSSIANS 1:18–2:7
PSALM 77:1-20
PROVERBS 24:23-25

Now, just as you accepted Christ Jesus as your Lord, you must continue to follow him. Let your roots grow down into him, and let your lives be built on him. Then your faith will grow strong in the truth you were taught, and you will overflow with thankfulness. **COLOSSIANS 2:6-7**

Ways I might encourage my child to grow deep roots in Christ:

My prayer for my child to grow strong in the truth he or she has been taught:

Other prayer concerns today:

October 6

JEREMIAH 6:16–8:7
COLOSSIANS 2:8-23
PSALM 78:1-31
PROVERBS 24:26

He issued his laws to Jacob;
he gave his instructions to Israel.
He commanded our ancestors
to teach them to their children,
so the next generation might know them—
even the children not yet born—
and they in turn will teach their own children.
So each generation should set its hope anew on God,
not forgetting his glorious miracles
and obeying his commands.
Then they will not be like their ancestors—
stubborn, rebellious, and unfaithful,
refusing to give their hearts to God.
PSALM 78:5-8

Ways I can make the Bible the central, all-permeating book in our home:

My prayer for my child to put his or her hope in God:

Other prayer concerns today:

October 7

JEREMIAH 8:8–9:26
COLOSSIANS 3:1-17
PSALM 78:32-55
PROVERBS 24:27

Since God chose you to be the holy people he loves, you must clothe yourselves with tenderhearted mercy, kindness, humility, gentleness, and patience. Make allowance for each other's faults, and forgive anyone who offends you. Remember, the Lord forgave you, so you must forgive others. Above all, clothe yourselves with love, which binds us all together in perfect harmony. And let the peace that comes from Christ rule in your hearts. For as members of one body you are called to live in peace. And always be thankful. **COLOSSIANS 3:12-15**

Situations in which I want to show greater kindness and gentleness in our home:

My prayer for greater forbearance, harmony, and peace in our home:

Other prayer concerns today:

October 8

JEREMIAH 10:1–11:23
COLOSSIANS 3:18–4:18
PSALM 78:56-72
PROVERBS 24:28-29

Wives, submit to your husbands, as is fitting for those who belong to the Lord. Husbands, love your wives and never treat them harshly. Children, always obey your parents, for this pleases the Lord. Fathers, do not aggravate your children, or they will become discouraged. **COLOSSIANS 3:18-21**

Specific ways I can affirm my child more and aggravate my child less:

My prayer for the ability to retrain parenting patterns that need to change:

Other prayer concerns today:

October 9

JEREMIAH 12:1–14:10
1 THESSALONIANS 1:1–2:8
PSALM 79:1-13
PROVERBS 24:30-34

The people say, "Our wickedness has caught up with us, LORD,
but help us for the sake of your own reputation.
We have turned away from you
and sinned against you again and again. . . .
We are known as your people.
Please don't abandon us now!"

JEREMIAH 14:7, 9

Things I long for God to do in our family that will demonstrate that he loves to save and generously gives grace:

My prayer for God to rain down his grace on our family:

Other prayer concerns today:

October 10

JEREMIAH 14:11–16:15
1 THESSALONIANS 2:9–3:13
PSALM 80:1-9
PROVERBS 25:1-5

We never stop thanking God that when you received his message from us, you didn't think of our words as mere human ideas. You accepted what we said as the very word of God—which, of course, it is. And this word continues to work in you who believe. **1 THESSALONIANS 2:13**

Areas where I need the Word to work in my life:

My prayer for the Word to work in my child's life:

Other prayer concerns today:

October 11

JEREMIAH 16:16–18:23
1 THESSALONIANS 4:1–5:3
PSALM 81:1-16
PROVERBS 25:6-8

The human heart is the most deceitful of all things,
and desperately wicked.
Who really knows how bad it is?
JEREMIAH 17:9

Desires I pray the Lord will instill in my child's heart:

My prayer for my child to instruct his or her heart to do what pleases God:

Other prayer concerns today:

October 12

JEREMIAH 19:1–21:14
1 THESSALONIANS 5:4-28
PSALM 82:1-8
PROVERBS 25:9-10

Never stop praying.
1 THESSALONIANS 5:17

Things I never want to give up praying for:

My prayer for greater dependence on God through prayer:

Other prayer concerns today:

October 13

JEREMIAH 22:1–23:20
2 THESSALONIANS 1:1-12
PSALM 83:1-18
PROVERBS 25:11-14

We keep on praying for you, asking our God to enable you to live a life worthy of his call. May he give you the power to accomplish all the good things your faith prompts you to do. Then the name of our Lord Jesus will be honored because of the way you live, and you will be honored along with him. This is all made possible because of the grace of our God and Lord, Jesus Christ. **2 THESSALONIANS 1:11-12**

Areas where I need God's spiritual power and resolve to do what he has called me to do:

My prayer that Christ will be honored in the way I parent:

Other prayer concerns today:

October 14

JEREMIAH 23:21–25:38
2 THESSALONIANS 2:1-17
PSALM 84:1-12
PROVERBS 25:15

This is what the LORD, *the God of Israel, said to me: "Take from my hand this cup filled to the brim with my anger, and make all the nations to whom I send you drink from it. When they drink from it, they will stagger, crazed by the warfare I will send against them."* **JEREMIAH 25:15-16**

My prayer for my child to drink of the cup of salvation rather than the cup of judgment:

My prayer of thanksgiving for Jesus' willingness to drink the cup that I deserve to drink:

Other prayer concerns today:

JEREMIAH 26:1–27:22
2 THESSALONIANS 3:1-18
PSALM 85:1-13
PROVERBS 25:16

October 15

Unfailing love and truth have met together.
Righteousness and peace have kissed!
PSALM 85:10

My prayer for my child to have peace with God:

My prayer for Christ's righteousness to become an increasing reality in my life and my child's life:

Other prayer concerns today:

October 16

JEREMIAH 28:1–29:32
1 TIMOTHY 1:1-20
PSALM 86:1-17
PROVERBS 25:17

I thank Christ Jesus our Lord, who has given me strength to do his work. He considered me trustworthy and appointed me to serve him, even though I used to blaspheme the name of Christ. In my insolence, I persecuted his people. But God had mercy on me because I did it in ignorance and unbelief. Oh, how generous and gracious our Lord was! He filled me with the faith and love that come from Christ Jesus. **1 TIMOTHY 1:12-14**

Areas where I need patience to trust in the timing of God's work in my child's life:

My prayer for faith to believe that my child's resistance is not beyond the patience of God:

Other prayer concerns today:

October 17

JEREMIAH 30:1–31:26
1 TIMOTHY 2:1-15
PSALM 87:1-7
PROVERBS 25:18-19

This is what the LORD says:
"Do not weep any longer,
for I will reward you," says the LORD.
"Your children will come back to you
from the distant land of the enemy.
There is hope for your future," says the LORD.
"Your children will come again to their own land.
I have heard Israel saying,
'You disciplined me severely,
like a calf that needs training for the yoke.
Turn me again to you and restore me,
for you alone are the LORD my God.'"

JEREMIAH 31:16-18

Ways I can tangibly demonstrate love to my child this week:

My prayer for my relationship with my child to be marked by loving discipline as well as abundant mercy:

Other prayer concerns today:

October 18

JEREMIAH 31:27–32:44
1 TIMOTHY 3:1-16
PSALM 88:1-18
PROVERBS 25:20-22

"This is the new covenant I will make with the people of Israel after those days," says the LORD. "I will put my instructions deep within them, and I will write them on their hearts. I will be their God, and they will be my people." **JEREMIAH 31:33**

My prayer for myself and my child to live out of the law of God written on our hearts:

My prayer for my child to be counted among those God calls "my people":

Other prayer concerns today:

October 19

JEREMIAH 33:1–34:22
1 TIMOTHY 4:1-16
PSALM 89:1-13
PROVERBS 25:23-24

"Physical training is good, but training for godliness is much better, promising benefits in this life and in the life to come." This is a trustworthy saying, and everyone should accept it. This is why we work hard and continue to struggle, for our hope is in the living God, who is the Savior of all people and particularly of all believers. **1 TIMOTHY 4:8-10**

Ways I pray my child will be willing to work hard and continue to struggle toward godliness:

My prayer for my child to see fruit in his or her efforts toward godliness:

Other prayer concerns today:

October 20

JEREMIAH 35:1–36:32
1 TIMOTHY 5:1-25
PSALM 89:14-37
PROVERBS 25:25-27

The king sent Jehudi to get the scroll. Jehudi brought it from Elishama's room and read it to the king as all his officials stood by. It was late autumn, and the king was in a winterized part of the palace, sitting in front of a fire to keep warm. Each time Jehudi finished reading three or four columns, the king took a knife and cut off that section of the scroll. He then threw it into the fire, section by section, until the whole scroll was burned up. Neither the king nor his attendants showed any signs of fear or repentance at what they heard. **JEREMIAH 36:21-24**

My prayer for God to protect my child from cynicism and rejection of the reliability and authority of the Bible:

My prayer for my child to have friends and teachers who help him or her to grow in respect and understanding of the Bible:

Other prayer concerns today:

October 21

JEREMIAH 37:1–38:28
1 TIMOTHY 6:1-21
PSALM 89:38-52
PROVERBS 25:28

True godliness with contentment is itself great wealth. After all, we brought nothing with us when we came into the world, and we can't take anything with us when we leave it. So if we have enough food and clothing, let us be content. **1 TIMOTHY 6:6-8**

Ways I can model contentment with "enough" in our home:

My prayer for me and my child to value spiritual wealth more than material wealth:

Other prayer concerns today:

October 22

JEREMIAH 39:1–41:18
2 TIMOTHY 1:1-18
PSALMS 90:1–91:16
PROVERBS 26:1-2

God has not given us a spirit of fear and timidity, but of power, love, and self-discipline. **2 TIMOTHY 1:7**

Fears that threaten to control me:

My prayer to parent out of confident hope in God's sovereign power and saving grace instead of out of fear:

Other prayer concerns today:

October 23

JEREMIAH 42:1–44:23
2 TIMOTHY 2:1-21
PSALMS 92:1–93:5
PROVERBS 26:3-5

Endure suffering along with me, as a good soldier of Christ Jesus. Soldiers don't get tied up in the affairs of civilian life, for then they cannot please the officer who enlisted them. And athletes cannot win the prize unless they follow the rules. And hardworking farmers should be the first to enjoy the fruit of their labor. **2 TIMOTHY 2:3-6**

My prayer for my child to be willing to endure suffering for his or her allegiance to Christ:

My prayer for my child to experience the joy of seeing the fruitfulness of gospel labors:

Other prayer concerns today:

October 24

JEREMIAH 44:24–47:7
2 TIMOTHY 2:22–3:17
PSALM 94:1-23
PROVERBS 26:6-8

Continue in what you have learned and have firmly believed, knowing from whom you learned it and how from childhood you have been acquainted with the sacred writings, which are able to make you wise for salvation through faith in Christ Jesus. All Scripture is breathed out by God and profitable for teaching, for reproof, for correction, and for training in righteousness, that the man of God may be complete, equipped for every good work. **2 TIMOTHY 3:14-17, ESV**

Ways I pray the Lord will use his Word in my child's life:

My prayer for the Scriptures to make my child wise for salvation through faith in Christ Jesus:

Other prayer concerns today:

October 25

JEREMIAH 48:1–49:22
2 TIMOTHY 4:1-22
PSALMS 95:1–96:13
PROVERBS 26:9-12

As for me, my life has already been poured out as an offering to God. The time of my death is near. I have fought the good fight, I have finished the race, and I have remained faithful. And now the prize awaits me—the crown of righteousness, which the Lord, the righteous Judge, will give me on the day of his return. And the prize is not just for me but for all who eagerly look forward to his appearing. **2 TIMOTHY 4:6-8**

Threats to staying in the fight for faith and finishing the race faithfully:

My prayer for perseverance over the long haul of my life:

Other prayer concerns today:

October 26

JEREMIAH 49:23–50:46
TITUS 1:1-16
PSALMS 97:1–98:9
PROVERBS 26:13-16

The LORD is king!
Let the earth rejoice!
Let the farthest coastlands be glad.
PSALM 97:1

Implications of knowing that King Jesus reigns over all:

My prayer of submission to Jesus as King over this world, our home, and my life:

Other prayer concerns today:

JEREMIAH 51:1-53
TITUS 2:1-15
PSALM 99:1-9
PROVERBS 26:17

October 27

As for you, Titus, promote the kind of living that reflects wholesome teaching. Teach the older men to exercise self-control, to be worthy of respect, and to live wisely. They must have sound faith and be filled with love and patience. Similarly, teach the older women to live in a way that honors God. They must not slander others or be heavy drinkers. Instead, they should teach others what is good. **TITUS 2:1-3**

How I'm doing regarding the instructions Paul gives in Titus 2:1-3:

My prayer to live in a way that is worthy of respect, a way that honors God:

Other prayer concerns today:

October 28

JEREMIAH 51:54–52:34
TITUS 3:1-15
PSALM 100:1-5
PROVERBS 26:18-19

Remind the believers to submit to the government and its officers. They should be obedient, always ready to do what is good. They must not slander anyone and must avoid quarreling. Instead, they should be gentle and show true humility to everyone. **TITUS 3:1-2**

What my child is likely picking up from me regarding submission to the government and its officers:

My prayer for restraint in my words and demeanor so that I don't slander anyone and avoid quarreling:

Other prayer concerns today:

October 29

LAMENTATIONS 1:1–2:22
PHILEMON 1:1-25
PSALM 101:1-8
PROVERBS 26:20

I will sing of your love and justice, Lord.
I will praise you with songs.
I will be careful to live a blameless life—
when will you come to help me?
I will lead a life of integrity
in my own home.
I will refuse to look at
anything vile and vulgar.
I hate all who deal crookedly;
I will have nothing to do with them.
I will reject perverse ideas
and stay away from every evil.
I will not tolerate people who slander their neighbors.
I will not endure conceit and pride.

PSALM 101:1-5

Areas in which I pray my child will live in integrity:

My prayer for my child to lead a life of integrity:

Other prayer concerns today:

October 30

LAMENTATIONS 3:1-66
HEBREWS 1:1-14
PSALM 102:1-28
PROVERBS 26:21-22

I will never forget this awful time,
as I grieve over my loss.
Yet I still dare to hope
when I remember this:
The faithful love of the LORD never ends!
His mercies never cease.
Great is his faithfulness;
his mercies begin afresh each morning.
I say to myself, "The LORD is my inheritance;
therefore, I will hope in him!"
LAMENTATIONS 3:20-24

Losses my child has experienced or may experience in the future:

My prayer for my child to dare to hope because of the goodness of the Lord:

Other prayer concerns today:

October 31

LAMENTATIONS 4:1–5:22
HEBREWS 2:1-18
PSALM 103:1-22
PROVERBS 26:23

Therefore, it was necessary for him to be made in every respect like us, his brothers and sisters, so that he could be our merciful and faithful High Priest before God. Then he could offer a sacrifice that would take away the sins of the people. Since he himself has gone through suffering and testing, he is able to help us when we are being tested. **HEBREWS 2:17-18**

Temptations my child faces that Jesus can help him or her with:

My prayer for my child to turn to Jesus for help when being tested by temptation:

Other prayer concerns today:

November 1

EZEKIEL 1:1–3:15
HEBREWS 3:1-19
PSALM 104:1-23
PROVERBS 26:24-26

"Son of man," he said, "I am sending you to the nation of Israel, a rebellious nation that has rebelled against me. They and their ancestors have been rebelling against me to this very day." **EZEKIEL 2:3**

The kind of parent my child needs more than a perfect parent:

My prayer for my child to receive the perfect obedience of Jesus as a gift:

Other prayer concerns today:

November 2

EZEKIEL 3:16–6:14
HEBREWS 4:1-16
PSALM 104:24-35
PROVERBS 26:27

The word of God is alive and powerful. It is sharper than the sharpest two-edged sword, cutting between soul and spirit, between joint and marrow. It exposes our innermost thoughts and desires. Nothing in all creation is hidden from God. Everything is naked and exposed before his eyes, and he is the one to whom we are accountable. **HEBREWS 4:12-13**

Ways I long for the Word to penetrate my child's innermost thoughts and desires:

My prayer for the life and power of God's Word to go to work in my child's life:

Other prayer concerns today:

November 3

EZEKIEL 7:1–9:11
HEBREWS 5:1-14
PSALM 105:1-15
PROVERBS 26:28

While Jesus was here on earth, he offered prayers and pleadings, with a loud cry and tears, to the one who could rescue him from death. And God heard his prayers because of his deep reverence for God. Even though Jesus was God's Son, he learned obedience from the things he suffered. In this way, God qualified him as a perfect High Priest, and he became the source of eternal salvation for all those who obey him. **HEBREWS 5:7-9**

Lessons I pray my child and I will learn from the suffering we experience:

My prayer for the grace to live in obedience to Christ even though it comes with a cost:

Other prayer concerns today:

November 4

EZEKIEL 10:1–11:25
HEBREWS 6:1-20
PSALM 105:16-36
PROVERBS 27:1-2

It is impossible to bring back to repentance those who were once enlightened—those who have experienced the good things of heaven and shared in the Holy Spirit, who have tasted the goodness of the word of God and the power of the age to come—and who then turn away from God. It is impossible to bring such people back to repentance; by rejecting the Son of God, they themselves are nailing him to the cross once again and holding him up to public shame. **HEBREWS 6:4-6**

My prayer for my child to take hold of all the goodness of the gospel that has been held out to him or her:

My prayer that my child will never turn away from God:

Other prayer concerns today:

November 5

EZEKIEL 12:1–14:11
HEBREWS 7:1-17
PSALM 105:37-45
PROVERBS 27:3

Jesus became a priest, not by meeting the physical requirement of belonging to the tribe of Levi, but by the power of a life that cannot be destroyed. **HEBREWS 7:16**

Needs I pray Jesus will intercede for before God's throne:

My prayer of gratitude for Jesus' ongoing intercession for me:

Other prayer concerns today:

November 6

EZEKIEL 14:12–16:41
HEBREWS 7:18-28
PSALM 106:1-12
PROVERBS 27:4-6

On the day you were born, you were unwanted, dumped in a field and left to die. But I came by and saw you there, helplessly kicking about in your own blood. As you lay there, I said, "Live!" And I helped you to thrive like a plant in the field. You grew up and became a beautiful jewel. **EZEKIEL 16:5-7**

My prayer of petition for God to declare "Live!" to my child and help him or her to thrive:

My prayer of praise to God for being a God who rescues the abandoned and loves the unlovable:

Other prayer concerns today:

November 7

EZEKIEL 16:42–17:24
HEBREWS 8:1-13
PSALM 106:13-31
PROVERBS 27:7-9

Now Jesus, our High Priest, has been given a ministry that is far superior to the old priesthood, for he is the one who mediates for us a far better covenant with God, based on better promises. **HEBREWS 8:6**

Aspects of the beauty of Christ I pray the Spirit will enable my child to see:

My prayer for my child to long for a genuine inner holiness:

Other prayer concerns today:

November 8

EZEKIEL 18:1–19:14
HEBREWS 9:1-10
PSALM 106:32-48
PROVERBS 27:10

The person who sins is the one who will die. The child will not be punished for the parent's sins, and the parent will not be punished for the child's sins. Righteous people will be rewarded for their own righteous behavior, and wicked people will be punished for their own wickedness. But if wicked people turn away from all their sins and begin to obey my decrees and do what is just and right, they will surely live and not die. All their past sins will be forgotten, and they will live because of the righteous things they have done. **EZEKIEL 18:20-22**

My own sins and failures I pray will not be repeated in my child's life:

My prayer of gratitude for knowing that my child is not destined to repeat my sins:

Other prayer concerns today:

November 9

EZEKIEL 20:1-49
HEBREWS 9:11-28
PSALM 107:1-43
PROVERBS 27:11

Under the old system, the blood of goats and bulls and the ashes of a heifer could cleanse people's bodies from ceremonial impurity. Just think how much more the blood of Christ will purify our consciences from sinful deeds so that we can worship the living God. For by the power of the eternal Spirit, Christ offered himself to God as a perfect sacrifice for our sins. **HEBREWS 9:13-14**

Areas in which my conscience sometimes bothers me:

My prayer for me and my child to experience the joy of a cleansed conscience after confession:

Other prayer concerns today:

EZEKIEL 21:1–22:31
HEBREWS 10:1-17
PSALM 108:1-13
PROVERBS 27:12

November 10

By one sacrifice he has made perfect forever those who are being made holy.

HEBREWS 10:14, NIV

Change and development I'm seeing in my children that I want to affirm:

My prayer for the gap between who I am by nature and who I've been declared to be in Christ to be increasingly closed:

Other prayer concerns today:

November 11

EZEKIEL 23:1-49
HEBREWS 10:18-39
PSALM 109:1-31
PROVERBS 27:13

Think back on those early days when you first learned about Christ. Remember how you remained faithful even though it meant terrible suffering. Sometimes you were exposed to public ridicule and were beaten, and sometimes you helped others who were suffering the same things. You suffered along with those who were thrown into jail, and when all you owned was taken from you, you accepted it with joy. You knew there were better things waiting for you that will last forever. **HEBREWS 10:32-34**

Better things waiting for me that will last forever:

My prayer to live before my child like I don't expect this world to ultimately satisfy me:

Other prayer concerns today:

November 12

EZEKIEL 24:1–26:21
HEBREWS 11:1-16
PSALM 110:1-7
PROVERBS 27:14

Faith shows the reality of what we hope for;
it is the evidence of things we cannot see.
HEBREWS 11:1

Things God has promised that I haven't yet seen or experienced but have confident hope I will:

My prayer for my child to have a countercultural confidence in what God has promised:

Other prayer concerns today:

November 13

EZEKIEL 27:1–28:26
HEBREWS 11:17-31
PSALM 111:1-10
PROVERBS 27:15-16

It was by faith that Moses, when he grew up, refused to be called the son of Pharaoh's daughter. He chose to share the oppression of God's people instead of enjoying the fleeting pleasures of sin. He thought it was better to suffer for the sake of Christ than to own the treasures of Egypt, for he was looking ahead to his great reward. **HEBREWS 11:24-26**

The eternal rewards I want for my child more than earthly pleasures and treasures:

My prayer for wisdom on how to help my child understand and value heavenly rewards:

Other prayer concerns today:

November 14

EZEKIEL 29:1–30:26
HEBREWS 11:32–12:13
PSALM 112:1-10
PROVERBS 27:17

Our earthly fathers disciplined us for a few years, doing the best they knew how. But God's discipline is always good for us, so that we might share in his holiness. No discipline is enjoyable while it is happening—it's painful! But afterward there will be a peaceful harvest of right living for those who are trained in this way. **HEBREWS 12:10-11**

Weaknesses I perceive in how I discipline my child:

My prayer for my child to be willing to be trained by God's discipline:

Other prayer concerns today:

November 15

EZEKIEL 31:1–32:32
HEBREWS 12:14-29
PSALMS 113:1–114:8
PROVERBS 27:18-20

Be careful that you do not refuse to listen to the One who is speaking. . . . When God spoke from Mount Sinai his voice shook the earth, but now he makes another promise: "Once again I will shake not only the earth but the heavens also." This means that all of creation will be shaken and removed, so that only unshakable things will remain. Since we are receiving a Kingdom that is unshakable, let us be thankful and please God by worshiping him with holy fear and awe. **HEBREWS 12:25-28**

Ways I've tried to create a secure life for my child:

My prayer for my child to experience perfect and eternal security by being joined to Christ:

Other prayer concerns today:

November 16

EZEKIEL 33:1–34:31
HEBREWS 13:1-25
PSALM 115:1-18
PROVERBS 27:21-22

Remember your leaders who taught you the word of God. Think of all the good that has come from their lives, and follow the example of their faith. **HEBREWS 13:7**

Leaders who have taught me and my child the Word of God for which I'm grateful:

My prayer for God to provide godly leaders to influence my child toward Christ:

Other prayer concerns today:

November 17

EZEKIEL 35:1–36:28
JAMES 1:1-18
PSALM 116:1-19
PROVERBS 27:23-27

Remember, when you are being tempted, do not say, "God is tempting me." God is never tempted to do wrong, and he never tempts anyone else. Temptation comes from our own desires, which entice us and drag us away. These desires give birth to sinful actions. And when sin is allowed to grow, it gives birth to death. **JAMES 1:13-15**

Temptations I pray my child will have the spiritual power to say no to:

My prayer for God to sanctify my child's desires:

Other prayer concerns today:

November 18

EZEKIEL 37:1–38:23
JAMES 1:19–2:17
PSALM 117:1-2
PROVERBS 28:1

Understand this, my dear brothers and sisters: You must all be quick to listen, slow to speak, and slow to get angry. Human anger does not produce the righteousness God desires. **JAMES 1:19-20**

Times when my anger has worked against the relationship I want to have with my child:

My prayer to be quick to listen, slow to speak, and slow to get angry:

Other prayer concerns today:

November 19

EZEKIEL 39:1–40:27
JAMES 2:18–3:18
PSALM 118:1-18
PROVERBS 28:2

The tongue is a small thing that makes grand speeches. But a tiny spark can set a great forest on fire. And among all the parts of the body, the tongue is a flame of fire. It is a whole world of wickedness, corrupting your entire body. It can set your whole life on fire, for it is set on fire by hell itself. **JAMES 3:5-6**

Ways I want to use my words to bless my child:

My prayer for God to cleanse from me what leads me to use my tongue to curse instead of bless:

Other prayer concerns today:

EZEKIEL 40:28–41:26
JAMES 4:1-17
PSALM 118:19-20
PROVERBS 28:3-5

November 20

You want what you don't have, so you scheme and kill to get it. You are jealous of what others have, but you can't get it, so you fight and wage war to take it away from them. Yet you don't have what you want because you don't ask God for it. And even when you ask, you don't get it because your motives are all wrong—you want only what will give you pleasure. **JAMES 4:2-3**

My confession of jealousy over what other families have or do:

My prayer for God to work in me so deeply that I not only do what is right, but do it with motives that please him:

Other prayer concerns today:

November 21

EZEKIEL 42:1–43:27
JAMES 5:1-20
PSALM 119:1-16
PROVERBS 28:6-7

Confess your sins to each other and pray for each other so that you may be healed. The earnest prayer of a righteous person has great power and produces wonderful results. **JAMES 5:16**

The last time I can remember confessing a specific sin to someone else:

My prayer for the humility to confess my sins to the people who will notice whether I change after confessing:

Other prayer concerns today:

November 22

EZEKIEL 44:1–45:12
1 PETER 1:1-12
PSALM 119:17-32
PROVERBS 28:8-10

All praise to God, the Father of our Lord Jesus Christ. It is by his great mercy that we have been born again, because God raised Jesus Christ from the dead. Now we live with great expectation, and we have a priceless inheritance—an inheritance that is kept in heaven for you, pure and undefiled, beyond the reach of change and decay. And through your faith, God is protecting you by his power until you receive this salvation, which is ready to be revealed on the last day for all to see. **1 PETER 1:3-5**

The inheritance that all who are in Christ can anticipate receiving when he returns:

My prayer for my child to value and receive this priceless inheritance:

Other prayer concerns today:

November 23

EZEKIEL 45:13–46:24
1 PETER 1:13–2:10
PSALM 119:33-48
PROVERBS 28:11

Preparing your minds for action, and being sober-minded, set your hope fully on the grace that will be brought to you at the revelation of Jesus Christ. As obedient children, do not be conformed to the passions of your former ignorance, but as he who called you is holy, you also be holy in all your conduct, since it is written, "You shall be holy, for I am holy." **1 PETER 1:13-16, ESV**

My prayer for my child to live not just for today but in light of his or her eternal destiny:

My prayer for my child to have a passion for holiness in a world that places no value on it:

Other prayer concerns today:

November 24

EZEKIEL 47:1–48:35
1 PETER 2:11–3:7
PSALM 119:49-64
PROVERBS 28:12-13

Don't be concerned about the outward beauty of fancy hairstyles, expensive jewelry, or beautiful clothes. You should clothe yourselves instead with the beauty that comes from within, the unfading beauty of a gentle and quiet spirit, which is so precious to God. **1 PETER 3:3-4**

Ways I can encourage my son or daughter to be more concerned about their quality of character than their physical attractiveness:

My prayer for myself and my child to desire the unfading beauty of a gentle and quiet spirit:

Other prayer concerns today:

November 25

DANIEL 1:1–2:23
1 PETER 3:8–4:6
PSALM 119:65-80
PROVERBS 28:14

The king ordered Ashpenaz, his chief of staff, to bring to the palace some of the young men of Judah's royal family and other noble families, who had been brought to Babylon as captives. "Select only strong, healthy, and good-looking young men," he said. "Make sure they are well versed in every branch of learning, are gifted with knowledge and good judgment, and are suited to serve in the royal palace. Train these young men in the language and literature of Babylon." **DANIEL 1:3-4**

What I want most in my child's education:

My prayer for my child to be aware of what can draw him or her away from allegiance to Christ:

Other prayer concerns today:

November 26

DANIEL 2:24–3:30
1 PETER 4:7–5:14
PSALM 119:81-96
PROVERBS 28:15-16

Shadrach, Meshach, and Abednego replied, "O Nebuchadnezzar, we do not need to defend ourselves before you. If we are thrown into the blazing furnace, the God whom we serve is able to save us. He will rescue us from your power, Your Majesty. But even if he doesn't, we want to make it clear to you, Your Majesty, that we will never serve your gods or worship the gold statue you have set up." **DANIEL 3:16-18**

Situations in which I find it difficult to be bold in my allegiance to Christ:

My prayer for myself and my child to have the courage to go against the crowd even when it may cost us:

Other prayer concerns today:

November 27

DANIEL 4:1-37
2 PETER 1:1-21
PSALM 119:97-112
PROVERBS 28:17-18

By his divine power, God has given us everything we need for living a godly life. We have received all of this by coming to know him, the one who called us to himself by means of his marvelous glory and excellence. And because of his glory and excellence, he has given us great and precious promises. These are the promises that enable you to share his divine nature and escape the world's corruption caused by human desires. **2 PETER 1:3-4**

What my child needs for living a godly life:

My prayer of gratitude to God for giving me and my child everything we need to live in a way that glorifies him:

Other prayer concerns today:

November 28

DANIEL 5:1-31
2 PETER 2:1-22
PSALM 119:113-128
PROVERBS 28:19-20

This is the message that was written: MENE, MENE, TEKEL, and PARSIN. . . . Tekel *means "weighed"—you have been weighed on the balances and have not measured up.* **DANIEL 5:25, 27**

What I deserve to have inscribed on the walls of my life and what is written instead by grace:

My prayer of gratitude for grace that covers all my failures as a parent:

Other prayer concerns today:

November 29

DANIEL 6:1-28
2 PETER 3:1-18
PSALM 119:129-152
PROVERBS 28:21-22

The Lord is not slow to fulfill his promise as some count slowness, but is patient toward you, not wishing that any should perish, but that all should reach repentance. **2 PETER 3:9, ESV**

My prayer of gratitude for the patience God has shown me:

My prayer welcoming God to work in my child's life on his timeline, not mine:

Other prayer concerns today:

November 30

DANIEL 7:1-28
1 JOHN 1:1-10
PSALM 119:153-176
PROVERBS 28:23-24

We proclaim to you the one who existed from the beginning, whom we have heard and seen. We saw him with our own eyes and touched him with our own hands. He is the Word of life. This one who is life itself was revealed to us, and we have seen him. And now we testify and proclaim to you that he is the one who is eternal life. He was with the Father, and then he was revealed to us. We proclaim to you what we ourselves have actually seen and heard so that you may have fellowship with us. And our fellowship is with the Father and with his Son, Jesus Christ. We are writing these things so that you may fully share our joy. **1 JOHN 1:1-4**

What it could look like to enjoy fellowship with my child as a brother or sister in Christ:

My prayer for Jesus to be the joy of my child's life:

Other prayer concerns today:

December 1

DANIEL 8:1-27
1 JOHN 2:1-17
PSALM 120:1-7
PROVERBS 28:25-26

Do not love this world nor the things it offers you, for when you love the world, you do not have the love of the Father in you. For the world offers only a craving for physical pleasure, a craving for everything we see, and pride in our achievements and possessions. These are not from the Father, but are from this world. And this world is fading away, along with everything that people crave. But anyone who does what pleases God will live forever. **1 JOHN 2:15-17**

What the world offers me and my child:

My prayer that we will not love the world in ways that diminish our love for Christ:

Other prayer concerns today:

December 2

DANIEL 9:1–11:1
1 JOHN 2:18–3:6
PSALM 121:1-8
PROVERBS 28:27-28

Since we know that Christ is righteous, we also know that all who do what is right are God's children. See how very much our Father loves us, for he calls us his children, and that is what we are! **1 JOHN 2:29–3:1**

Ways I can encourage my child's efforts toward holy living:

My prayer for my life and my child's life to increasingly reflect the righteousness of Christ:

Other prayer concerns today:

December 3

We know what real love is because Jesus gave up his life for us. **1 JOHN 3:16**

DANIEL 11:2-35
1 JOHN 3:7-24
PSALM 122:1-9
PROVERBS 29:1

How I think I'm doing at expressing love to my child in meaningful ways:

My prayer for the love of Christ to flow through me toward my child:

Other prayer concerns today:

December 4

DANIEL 11:36–12:13
1 JOHN 4:1-21
PSALM 123:1-4
PROVERBS 29:2-4

Dear friends, do not believe everyone who claims to speak by the Spirit. You must test them to see if the spirit they have comes from God. For there are many false prophets in the world. This is how we know if they have the Spirit of God: If a person claiming to be a prophet acknowledges that Jesus Christ came in a real body, that person has the Spirit of God. **1 JOHN 4:1-2**

Voices about who Christ is and what he requires that have a hearing in my child's life:

My prayer for wisdom on how to challenge the voices my child listens to that don't conform to Scripture:

Other prayer concerns today:

December 5

HOSEA 1:1–3:5
1 JOHN 5:1-21
PSALM 124:1-8
PROVERBS 29:5-8

We know that God's children do not make a practice of sinning, for God's Son holds them securely, and the evil one cannot touch them. **1 JOHN 5:18**

Concerns I have about my child's safety:

My prayer to have greater confidence in the security provided to my child in Christ:

Other prayer concerns today:

December 6

HOSEA 4:1–5:15
2 JOHN 1:1-13
PSALM 125:1-5
PROVERBS 29:9-11

Those who trust in the LORD are as secure as Mount Zion;
they will not be defeated but will endure forever.
Just as the mountains surround Jerusalem,
so the LORD surrounds his people, both now and forever.
PSALM 125:1-2

What it means to me to know that the Lord surrounds his people:

My prayer of trust in the Lord to be my child's security and protection:

Other prayer concerns today:

December 7

HOSEA 6:1–9:17
3 JOHN 1:1-15
PSALM 126:1-6
PROVERBS 29:12-14

This letter is from John, the elder. I am writing to Gaius, my dear friend, whom I love in the truth. Dear friend, I hope all is well with you and that you are as healthy in body as you are strong in spirit. Some of the traveling teachers recently returned and made me very happy by telling me about your faithfulness and that you are living according to the truth. I could have no greater joy than to hear that my children are following the truth. **3 JOHN 1:1-4**

My level of comfort in asking my child about his or her spiritual health:

My prayer for my child's physical and spiritual health:

Other prayer concerns today:

December 8

HOSEA 10:1–14:9
JUDE 1:1-25
PSALM 127:1-5
PROVERBS 29:15-17

Now all glory to God, who is able to keep you from falling away and will bring you with great joy into his glorious presence without a single fault. All glory to him who alone is God, our Savior through Jesus Christ our Lord. All glory, majesty, power, and authority are his before all time, and in the present, and beyond all time! Amen. **JUDE 1:24-25**

All the things my child may experience through which God is able to keep him or her:

My prayer for my child to keep himself or herself in the love of God:

Other prayer concerns today:

December 9

JOEL 1:1–3:21
REVELATION 1:1-20
PSALM 128:1-6
PROVERBS 29:18

The threshing floors shall be full of grain;
the vats shall overflow with wine and oil.
I will restore to you the years
that the swarming locust has eaten.
JOEL 2:24-25, ESV

Areas of regret to which I pray the Lord will bring restoration:

My prayer asking the Lord for restoration:

Other prayer concerns today:

December 10

AMOS 1:1–3:15
REVELATION 2:1-17
PSALM 129:1-8
PROVERBS 29:19-20

I know all the things you do. I have seen your hard work and your patient endurance. I know you don't tolerate evil people. You have examined the claims of those who say they are apostles but are not. You have discovered they are liars. You have patiently suffered for me without quitting. But I have this complaint against you. You don't love me or each other as you did at first! Look how far you have fallen! Turn back to me and do the works you did at first. **REVELATION 2:2-5**

Things I did when my love for Christ was new:

My prayer for freshness in my love for Christ:

Other prayer concerns today:

December 11

AMOS 4:1–6:14
REVELATION 2:18–3:6
PSALM 130:1-8
PROVERBS 29:21-22

What sorrow awaits you who say,
"If only the day of the LORD were here!"
You have no idea what you are wishing for.
That day will bring darkness, not light.
AMOS 5:18

Reasons for anticipation and/or dread of the Day of the Lord (when Jesus returns to earth):

My prayer for everyone in our family to be able to anticipate the Day of the Lord with gladness:

Other prayer concerns today:

December 12

AMOS 7:1–9:15
REVELATION 3:7-22
PSALM 131:1-3
PROVERBS 29:23

Then he showed me another vision. I saw the Lord standing beside a wall that had been built using a plumb line. He was using a plumb line to see if it was still straight. And the LORD said to me, "Amos, what do you see?" I answered, "A plumb line." And the Lord replied, "I will test my people with this plumb line. I will no longer ignore all their sins." **AMOS 7:7-8**

Standards or expectations (spoken and unspoken) I've set for my child:

My prayer to give my child the kind of grace I've received from God over my failure to live up to his standards:

Other prayer concerns today:

December 13

OBADIAH 1:1-21
REVELATION 4:1-11
PSALM 132:1-18
PROVERBS 29:24-25

As I looked, I saw a door standing open in heaven, and the same voice I had heard before spoke to me like a trumpet blast. The voice said, "Come up here, and I will show you what must happen after this." And instantly I was in the Spirit, and I saw a throne in heaven and someone sitting on it. **REVELATION 4:1-2**

Ways I can communicate to my child that everything in our lives revolves around God, not us:

My prayer for my child to make Jesus Christ the focal point of life and the source of joy:

Other prayer concerns today:

December 14

JONAH 1:1–4:11
REVELATION 5:1-14
PSALM 133:1-3
PROVERBS 29:26-27

My salvation comes from the L*ORD alone.*
JONAH 2:9

Reasons "salvation comes from the LORD alone" is good news:

My prayer for the Lord to save:

Other prayer concerns today:

December 15

MICAH 1:1–4:13
REVELATION 6:1-17
PSALM 134:1-3
PROVERBS 30:1-4

Then everyone—the kings of the earth, the rulers, the generals, the wealthy, the powerful, and every slave and free person—all hid themselves in the caves and among the rocks of the mountains. And they cried to the mountains and the rocks, "Fall on us and hide us from the face of the one who sits on the throne and from the wrath of the Lamb. For the great day of their wrath has come, and who is able to survive?" **REVELATION 6:15-17**

Extended family members and friends I pray will see their need to be covered by the blood of the Lamb:

My prayer that my child will be protected by the Lamb's presence for all eternity:

Other prayer concerns today:

MICAH 5:1–7:20
REVELATION 7:1-17
PSALM 135:1-21
PROVERBS 30:5-6

December 16

What can we bring to the LORD?
Should we bring him burnt offerings?
Should we bow before God Most High
with offerings of yearling calves?
Should we offer him thousands of rams
and ten thousand rivers of olive oil?
Should we sacrifice our firstborn children
to pay for our sins?

MICAH 6:6-7

Evidence that justice, mercy, and walking humbly with God are valued in our home:

My prayer for the Spirit to stir in us a greater passion for justice, mercy, and walking humbly with God:

Other prayer concerns today:

December 17

NAHUM 1:1–3:19
REVELATION 8:1-13
PSALM 136:1-26
PROVERBS 30:7-9

O God, I beg two favors from you;
let me have them before I die.
First, help me never to tell a lie.
Second, give me neither poverty nor riches!
Give me just enough to satisfy my needs.
For if I grow rich, I may deny you and say, "Who is the LORD?"
And if I am too poor, I may steal and thus insult God's holy name.
PROVERBS 30:7-9

Conversations we should have about money:

My prayer that my child's financial life will bring glory to God:

Other prayer concerns today:

HABAKKUK 1:1–3:19
REVELATION 9:1-21
PSALM 137:1-9
PROVERBS 30:10

December 18

I trembled inside when I heard this;
my lips quivered with fear.
My legs gave way beneath me,
and I shook in terror.
I will wait quietly for the coming day
when disaster will strike the people who invade us.
Even though the fig trees have no blossoms,
and there are no grapes on the vines;
even though the olive crop fails,
and the fields lie empty and barren;
even though the flocks die in the fields,
and the cattle barns are empty,
yet I will rejoice in the LORD!
I will be joyful in the God of my salvation!

HABAKKUK 3:16-18

My declaration of determination to rejoice in the Lord even though loss invades our lives:

My prayer for the faith to trust that God will preserve us through loss and harm:

Other prayer concerns today:

December 19

ZEPHANIAH 1:1–3:20
REVELATION 10:1-11
PSALM 138:1-8
PROVERBS 30:11-14

On that day the announcement to Jerusalem will be,
"Cheer up, Zion! Don't be afraid!
For the LORD your God is living among you.
He is a mighty savior.
He will take delight in you with gladness.
With his love, he will calm all your fears.
He will rejoice over you with joyful songs."
ZEPHANIAH 3:16-17

Ways I can communicate to my child the delight the Lord has over people:

My prayer for our family to experience the joy of the Lord's delight in us:

Other prayer concerns today:

December 20

HAGGAI 1:1–2:23
REVELATION 11:1-19
PSALM 139:1-24
PROVERBS 30:15-16

"This is what the LORD of Heaven's Armies says: The people are saying, 'The time has not yet come to rebuild the house of the LORD.'" Then the LORD sent this message through the prophet Haggai: "Why are you living in luxurious houses while my house lies in ruins?" **HAGGAI 1:2-4**

Ways our family is investing in building his Kingdom in the world:

My prayer for our family to be used in building Christ's Kingdom:

Other prayer concerns today:

December 21

ZECHARIAH 1:1-21
REVELATION 12:1-17
PSALM 140:1-13
PROVERBS 30:17

Then I heard a loud voice shouting across the heavens,

"It has come at last—
salvation and power
and the Kingdom of our God,
and the authority of his Christ.
For the accuser of our brothers and sisters
has been thrown down to earth—
the one who accuses them
before our God day and night.
And they have defeated him by the blood of the Lamb
and by their testimony."

REVELATION 12:10-11

My prayer of thanksgiving that my past sins and failures are no longer held against me:

My prayer of petition for my child to experience the freedom of forgiveness from God:

Other prayer concerns today:

December 22

ZECHARIAH 2:1–3:10
REVELATION 12:18–13:18
PSALM 141:1-10
PROVERBS 30:18-20

Hear now, O Joshua the high priest, you and your friends who sit before you, for they are men who are a sign: behold, I will bring my servant the Branch. For behold, on the stone that I have set before Joshua, on a single stone with seven eyes, I will engrave its inscription, declares the LORD of hosts, and I will remove the iniquity of this land in a single day. **ZECHARIAH 3:8-9, ESV**

Ways we can point to the purpose of Christ's coming during this season:

My prayer for our family to value the sacrifice of Jesus in this season of giving:

Other prayer concerns today:

December 23

ZECHARIAH 4:1–5:11
REVELATION 14:1-20
PSALM 142:1-7
PROVERBS 30:21-23

I saw the Lamb standing on Mount Zion, and with him were 144,000 who had his name and his Father's name written on their foreheads. **REVELATION 14:1**

Evidences I'd like to see in my child's life that he or she belongs to Christ:

My prayer of longing to one day gather as a complete family around the throne of God:

Other prayer concerns today:

December 24

ZECHARIAH 6:1–7:14
REVELATION 15:1-8
PSALM 143:1-12
PROVERBS 30:24-28

Let me hear of your unfailing love each morning,
for I am trusting you.
Show me where to walk,
for I give myself to you.
PSALM 143:8

Areas I need divine direction in how to best parent my child:

My prayer for rescue from discouragement and fear over my child's future:

Other prayer concerns today:

December 25

ZECHARIAH 8:1-23
REVELATION 16:1-21
PSALM 144:1-15
PROVERBS 30:29-31

Among the other nations, Judah and Israel became symbols of a cursed nation. But no longer! Now I will rescue you and make you both a symbol and a source of blessing. So don't be afraid. Be strong, and get on with rebuilding the Temple! **ZECHARIAH 8:13**

People in our lives to whom we want to be a conduit of the blessing of Christ:

My prayer for our family to be used to draw others to Christ:

Other prayer concerns today:

ZECHARIAH 9:1-17
REVELATION 17:1-18
PSALM 145:1-21
PROVERBS 30:32

December 26

Rejoice, O people of Zion!
Shout in triumph, O people of Jerusalem!
Look, your king is coming to you.
He is righteous and victorious,
yet he is humble, riding on a donkey—
riding on a donkey's colt.
ZECHARIAH 9:9

My list of reasons to praise God for the kind of King he's provided to us in Jesus:

My prayer for Jesus to overcome all resistance and rebellion in my child's life:

Other prayer concerns today:

December 27

ZECHARIAH 10:1–11:17
REVELATION 18:1-24
PSALM 146:1-10
PROVERBS 30:33

I will strengthen Judah and save Israel;
I will restore them because of my compassion.
It will be as though I had never rejected them,
for I am the LORD their God, who will hear their cries.
The people of Israel will become like mighty warriors,
and their hearts will be made happy as if by wine.
Their children, too, will see it and be glad;
their hearts will rejoice in the LORD.
When I whistle to them, they will come running,
for I have redeemed them.
ZECHARIAH 10:6-8

The things and people the Good Shepherd used to call me to himself:

My prayer for my child to come running when Jesus calls him or her:

Other prayer concerns today:

December 28

ZECHARIAH 12:1–13:9
REVELATION 19:1-21
PSALM 147:1-20
PROVERBS 31:1-7

On that day a fountain will be opened for the dynasty of David and for the people of Jerusalem, a fountain to cleanse them from all their sins and impurity. **ZECHARIAH 13:1**

My prayer for my sin and my child's sin to be purged and cleansed by the blood of Christ:

My prayer for passive rebellion and spiritual apathy to be a thing of the past in my life and my child's life:

Other prayer concerns today:

December 29

ZECHARIAH 14:1-21
REVELATION 20:1-15
PSALM 148:1-14
PROVERBS 31:8-9

I saw the dead, both great and small, standing before God's throne. And the books were opened, including the Book of Life. And the dead were judged according to what they had done, as recorded in the books. . . . And anyone whose name was not found recorded in the Book of Life was thrown into the lake of fire. **REVELATION 20:12, 15**

What I'd like the books to say about my life when they are opened:

My prayer for my child's name to be found recorded in the Book of Life:

Other prayer concerns today:

December 30

MALACHI 1:1–2:17
REVELATION 21:1-27
PSALM 149:1-9
PROVERBS 31:10-24

He took me in the Spirit to a great, high mountain, and he showed me the holy city, Jerusalem, descending out of heaven from God. . . . The city wall was broad and high, with twelve gates guarded by twelve angels. And the names of the twelve tribes of Israel were written on the gates. There were three gates on each side—east, north, south, and west. The wall of the city had twelve foundation stones, and on them were written the names of the twelve apostles of the Lamb. **REVELATION 21:10, 12-14**

What I know about the twelve tribes and twelve apostles that gives me hope for our family to be a part of God's eternal Holy City:

My prayer for Jesus to come and welcome our entire family into his Holy City:

Other prayer concerns today:

December 31

MALACHI 3:1–4:6
REVELATION 22:1-21
PSALM 150:1-6
PROVERBS 31:25-31

Look, I am sending you the prophet Elijah before the great and dreadful day of the LORD arrives. His preaching will turn the hearts of fathers to their children, and the hearts of children to their fathers. Otherwise I will come and strike the land with a curse. **MALACHI 4:5-6**

My prayer for reconciliation where there is alienation and relationship where there is estrangement:

My prayer for softened hearts toward each other in our home:

Other prayer concerns today:

ANSWERS TO PRAYER

ANSWERS TO PRAYER

ANSWERS TO PRAYER

ANSWERS TO PRAYER

ANSWERS TO PRAYER

ANSWERS TO PRAYER

ANSWERS TO PRAYER

ANSWERS TO PRAYER

About the Author

Nancy Guthrie teaches the Bible at her home church, Cornerstone Presbyterian Church in Franklin, Tennessee, as well as at conferences around the country and internationally, including her Biblical Theology Workshop for Women. She has a masters of theological studies from Reformed Theological Seminary and is the host of the *Help Me Teach the Bible* podcast with The Gospel Coalition. She and her husband, David, are the parents of three children, two of whom are with the Lord. They founded Respite Retreats for couples who have faced the death of a child, and they are cohosts of the GriefShare video series.

BY NANCY GUTHRIE

Holding On to Hope

The One Year™ Book of Hope Devotional

Hearing Jesus Speak into Your Sorrow

When Your Family's Lost a Loved One (with David Guthrie)

What Grieving People Wish You Knew about What Really Helps (and What Really Hurts)

One Year™ of Dinner Table Devotions and Discussion Starters

The One Year™ Discovering Jesus in the Old Testament Devotional

Abundant Life in Jesus

The One Year™ Praying through the Bible for Your Kids

God Does His Best Work with Empty

Seeing Jesus

What Every Child Should Know about Prayer

All Is Bright

Hoping for Something Better

Let Every Heart Prepare Him Room

CP1149